Britain and the Berlin Crisis, 1961

Britain and the Berlin Crisis, 1961

Edited by Richard Smith

Documents from the British Archives: No. 3

Documents from the British Archives: a thematic series with documents drawn from, or supplementing, volumes of *Documents on British Policy Overseas*, produced by the Foreign, Commonwealth and Development Office Historians.

Series editors: Patrick Salmon & Richard Smith

This publication is available online: www.issuu.com/fcohistorians

Cover illustration: Berlin Wall. British guards along the Brandenburg Gate
Credit: Allied Museum Berlin/© US Army

ISBN: 9798516680199

CONTENTS

Above: Berlin Wall demonstrations, Potsdamer Platz, August 1961. *Below*: Construction of the Wall at Wildenbruch Strasse, August 1961 (Allied Museum Berlin/© US Army).

INTRODUCTION

Early on the morning of 13 August 1961, East German border guards began to set up barbed wire barriers in the middle of Berlin, dividing the Soviet sector in the east from the British, French and American sectors in the west. The barbed wire was soon replaced by a wall of concrete blocks. The barrier became known as the Berlin Wall, and would remain the most visible symbol of the Cold War and the division of Europe until it was breached dramatically on the night of 9 November 1989. The documents in this volume describe events as they unfolded, during the initial stages of the crisis, from the perspective of British diplomats and military personnel on the ground in Berlin, and in the context of international diplomacy playing out between Britain, France, the USA—and the Soviet Union.[1]

The construction of the Berlin Wall was the culmination of a three year crisis over the question of the city's status. In November 1958, Soviet leader Nikita Khrushchev issued a demand that Berlin become a demilitarised free city with the withdrawal of the four Powers—the USA, USSR, Great Britain and France. West Berlin, a capitalist outpost behind the iron curtain, was an increasing irritant to Communist authorities. The democratic, liberal and increasingly prosperous West German state drew a steady flow of refugees from the East. Most took advantage of the relatively open borders in Berlin compared with the more heavily policed national borders of the German Democratic Republic (GDR). Between the establishment of the communist régime in East Germany in September 1949 and 31 May 1961, over 2.6 million people left the GDR. Their loss was a costly drain on the economy, and both the East German and Soviet leadership increasingly saw Berlin as the key to resolving the problem. Khrushchev threatened to sign a separate peace treaty with the GDR if no agreement was reached within six months, ending the occupation of East Berlin by Soviet forces and the quadripartite agreements that guaranteed US, British and French rights of access to West Berlin. This would make access dependent on the GDR, a country the Western powers did not even recognise. They rejected Khrushchev's demands, standing by the legal

---

[1] Documents relating to the fall of the Berlin Wall in 1989 can be found in *Documents on British Policy Overseas*: K. Hamilton, P. Salmon, S. Twigge (eds.), Series 3, Volume 7, *German Unification, 1989-1990* (London: Routledge, 2009) and R. Smith (ed.) Series 3, Volume 12, *Britain and the Revolutions in Eastern Europe, 1989* (London: Routledge, 2020).

basis of their presence in Berlin and warning the Russians of the dangers of attempting to unilaterally terminate Western rights, but they did agree to begin talks on the issue. These continued, without reaching any conclusion, until 1961 when Khrushchev reissued his ultimatum at a superpower summit in Vienna on 4 June. By this time Cold War tensions had been heightened by the Communist takeover of Cuba by Fidel Castro in 1959, the downing of the U-2 reconnaissance aircraft over Soviet territory in May 1960, increasing superpower involvement in the conflict in Laos, and the failed CIA backed 'Bay of Pigs' invasion of Cuba in April 1961. The Western powers formed a military planning group, LIVE OAK, to prepare contingency plans to respond to any interference with free access to West Berlin. The Americans favoured despatching forces along the Autobahn in the event of Soviet or East German action, and, if that failed, an airlift. Berlin, once again, threatened to ignite the Cold War.

In early August 1961, the flow of refugees into West Berlin from the East reached levels unparalleled since the East German rising of 1953, with 20,000 fleeing to the West in less than a fortnight. The sharp increase was of considerable concern to British diplomats. They recognised that its primary cause was probably a fear that the escape route might soon be closed. Migration seemed bound to damage the economy of the GDR and its prestige abroad, and there was an 'obvious danger' that East German attempts to stem the tide could 'complicate the Berlin problem still further and possibly even precipitate a crisis' (No. 3). Bernard Ledwidge, Political Adviser to the British Military Government in Berlin (BMG), even speculated on the 'remote contingency' of civil disturbances in East Germany similar to those of 1953 (No. 2). But in a telegram of 12 August, a day on which the record daily number of 2,400 crossed from East to West, the BMG reported that it did not consider that the population movement would itself precipitate an acute crisis. 'Rather', the BMG concluded, 'we should say that the state of affairs within East Germany increases for Khrushchev the attractiveness of some agreement with the Western Powers as against a unilaterally imposed "settlement" of the German problem' (No. 4).

Early on the morning of 13 August 1961, the GDR Government announced new and much stricter controls on the movement of East Germans, including East Berliners, to West Berlin, and proceeded to erect barricades sealing off the Soviet from the Western sectors of the city (No. 5). The first indication that anything was amiss came just after midnight, from a military police patrol who reported seeing great numbers of East German soldiers assembling. Brigadier L.F. Richards, in charge of military police operations in Berlin, drove to the Brandenburg Gate where he saw the border being blocked off with concrete blocks and barbed wire, and columns of vehicles unloading police, soldiers and engineering stores 'as far as the eye could see'. He crossed into East Berlin: 'It was a scene of great and intense activity: I could feel considerable tension. There were uniformed men everywhere, all heavily armed. Almost every open space of ground had military vehicles of one sort or another on it.' The main roads 'were jammed; packed with military vehicles including armoured vehicles and a lot of transport vehicles carrying barbed wire and other materials'. The few civilians he saw in East Berlin seemed 'bewildered and apprehensive'. By the end of the day, there was a physical barrier along the 26 miles of the British section of the zonal border. As all the activity was on the East German side of the demarcation line the British authorities had no cause to intervene. The West Berliners thought differently and started to demonstrate in their tens of thousands, hurling abuse and missiles at the East German working parties.[2]

In this potentially dangerous situation the British Government was concerned 'that nothing should be said or done by the West to increase the tension or to stimulate uprising in East Germany' (No. 10). The British Foreign Secretary, Lord Home, was reluctant to engage in any action by the Western powers which might invite counter-measures and allow events to escalate out of control. Even a West German proposal for suspending the issue of Temporary Travel Documents (TTDs) to East German citizens was initially opposed on the grounds that, since the GDR was unlikely to lift its latest restrictions, the suspension would become permanent (No. 9). Indeed, Home was inclined to see in the East German move a possible 'peg on which to hang a proposal for talks' leading, he hoped, to a negotiated arrangement which would guarantee the Western position in Berlin and the freedom and viability of West Berlin itself (No. 13). However, agreement was reached at a meeting in Washington on the evening of 15 August between the British, French and West German Ambassadors there and Foy Kohler, the US Assistant Secretary of State for European Affairs (the Ambassadorial Group), on the text of Notes, delivered separately in Moscow on 17 August by the Ambassadors of the three Western occupying powers, protesting at the 'flagrant, and particularly serious, violation of the quadripartite status of Berlin' (Nos. 15-17). Faced by mounting criticism, particularly in Germany, of Western inaction, Home was also ready at Washington's behest to undertake certain military measures, including the reinforcement of the British garrison in

---

[2] Recollections of Brigadier L.F. Richards (given at a witness seminar on British policy and the Berlin Wall Crisis held at King's College on 22 March 1991 under the auspices of the Department of War Studies and the Institute of Contemporary British History), published in John P. S. Gearson, 'British policy and the Berlin Wall crisis 1958–61', *Contemporary British History*, Vol. 6, No. 1 (1992), pp. 153-7.

Berlin and participation in hastening the build-up of NATO forces (No. 23).

The Americans were disappointed that the reinforcement of British forces in Berlin consisted of no more than the despatch of armoured vehicles to the city (No. 32). They, like the French, were similarly perturbed over the Foreign Office's desire to link a proposed statement by the three Western Heads of Government, affirming their determination to maintain their rights and fulfil their obligations in Berlin, to messages to the Soviet Government indicating their readiness to explore the 'modalities of negotiations' (Nos. 28, 29, 32). But from Moscow the British Ambassador, Sir Frank Roberts, warned Home against a tripartite declaration which might provoke further action or some violent counter-declaration by Khrushchev. Roberts thought it important to 'guard against the danger that the exercise of reassuring the Berliners and maintaining West German morale might take us so far that it forced a response from Khrushchev which would still further increase tension and involve us all in political and possibly military escalation' (No. 33). With this Home evidently agreed. Certainly, he found unacceptable de Gaulle's opinion that a move towards negotiations would be inconsistent with the tough tone of the draft statement, and, in view of divergent British and French views on this issue, Kennedy decided to abandon the tripartite statement (No. 35). West Berliners had meanwhile to make do with a visit from the US Vice-President, Lyndon Johnson, and the despatch to the city of an American battle group. There was no point, the British ambassador in Bonn, Sir Christopher Steel, noted in a telegram of 21 August, 'in further bolstering Berlin morale, which [was] far too addicted to a diet of gestures' (No. 37). Nor was Steel ready to take too seriously a Soviet Note of 23 August protesting at the connivance of the Western allies with West German '[r]evanchists, extremists, subverters, spies and saboteurs' who had been allowed to use their air corridors to Berlin. He estimated that any physical action in the air corridor would appear to Khrushchev as being 'about the most dangerous he could take', and he dismissed the Note as part of the general propaganda build-up, designed 'to create a new factitious grievance with an eye to coming negotiations' (Nos. 38 & 42).

That there would be negotiations Home seems not to have doubted. In a Cabinet memorandum of 1 September he predicted a 'very tough and difficult' negotiation before the end of the year. To that end he supported Kennedy's efforts to increase American military preparedness and measures to strengthen NATO (No. 43). In fact, however, with the sealing off of East from West Berlin the prospect of negotiations receded. On 17 October, at the Soviet Communist Party Congress, Khrushchev withdrew his deadline for the signing of a peace treaty,[3] and for the time being there were no public references by the East German leader, Walter Ulbricht, to the transformation of West Berlin into a neutralised free city. As Steel subsequently noted, the construction of a wall separating East from West 'removed a great deal of Berlin's sting from the Soviet point of view'.[4] Nonetheless, the Berlin wall by no means solved the problems of the GDR, and the divided city remained a potential source of conflict. 'The continuous survival of West Berlin as a thriving outpost of the Western world in the middle of the DDR must', observed Major-General Rohan Delacombe, the General Officer Commanding the British sector, 'be regarded by Herr Ulbricht as an intolerable obstacle to his regime's consolidation and as a permanently unsettling factor. The reflection of the bright lights of West Berlin is still visible even across the Wall, the very existence of which enhances the poignancy and attractiveness of the sight.'[5]

The documents in this book are largely drawn from *Documents on British Policy Overseas (DBPO): Berlin in the Cold War, 1948-1990.*[6] This was one of two DBPO volumes produced in a hybrid semi-electronic format rather than in traditional hard copy. It consisted of facsimile reproduction of over 500 documents on CD Rom within a hard copy companion volume, which included editorial material. The intention was to make records available quickly and more cheaply. However, it was a classic case of investing in technology that seemed permanent at the time only to see its usability fade relatively quickly. Documents were captured on disks that can no longer be easily read. For this reason, we have chosen to reproduce a selection, relating to the United Kingdom's response to the Berlin Crisis of 1961, on the occasion of the 60th anniversary.

Richard Smith

---

[3] Cmnd. 6201, *Selected Documents on Germany and the Question of Berlin 1963-1973* (London: HMSO, 1975), pp. 36-37.

[4] FRG: Annual Review 1961, Bonn despatch No. 1 of 2 January 1962, CG 1011/1.

[5] Review of Developments in East Germany in 1961, GOC Berlin despatch No. 7 E(S) to Bonn of 8 March 1962, CG 1011/2.

[6] Keith Hamilton, Patrick Salmon, Stephen Twigge (eds.), *Documents on British Policy Overseas*, Series 3, Volume 6, *Berlin in the Cold War, 1948-1990* (London: Routledge, 2009).

BERLIN 1961

Sir Stephen Barrett KCMG joined the Foreign Office in 1955. His postings included: Political Office with Middle East Forces, Cyprus, 1957–59; Deputy Political Adviser, Berlin, 1959–62; Head of Chancery, Helsinki, 1965-68; Counsellor, Prague, 1972–74; Head of South West European Department, FCO, later Principal Private Secretary to the Secretary of State for Foreign and Commonwealth Affairs, 1975; Head of Science and Technology Department, FCO, 1976-77; Counsellor, Ankara, 1978–81; Head of British Interests Section, Tehran, 1981; Assistant Under-Secretary of State, FCO, 1981–84; Ambassador to Czechoslovakia, 1985–88; and Ambassador to Poland, 1988–91.[1]

I was Deputy Political Adviser in the British Military Government Berlin from 1959 to 1962. In August 1961 I was 29 years old. In Berlin, my responsibilities centred round the quadripartite status of the city, access between Berlin and the Federal Republic of Germany and movement within Berlin as a whole. This covered movement by land, air, railroads and water. I knew well as colleagues and friends my American and French opposite numbers as well as senior officers in the British military in Berlin. The personal reflections and comments that follow are in no way representative of an official view.

Events on 13 August and the following days

I was alerted to the beginning of the East German operation early in the afternoon of Sunday August 13. Later that day on the orders of the British Commandant a troop of British tanks went to the eastern end of the Strasse des 17 Juni, stopping some tens of yards short of the end of the British Sector where the East Germans were putting in place the early barricades to the west of the Brandenburg Gate. These were probably the first Western tanks to go up to the sector border between West and East Berlin.

---

[1] These recollections were made in 2011.

It was done to show some Western response and bolster West Berlin morale. Later that day I went to where our tanks were positioned and had a conversation with Senator Lipschitz (responsible in the West Berlin government for internal security and police matters). He pressed me hard on the need for a firm Western response.

A day or so later the British Commandant ordered that barbed wire should be placed around the Soviet war memorial in the Tiergarten. This was partly to show opposition to the barriers going up between East and West Berlin and partly to protect the memorial and the Soviet guards there against possible action by angry West Berliners. At any rate the Soviets hated it and a few days later I had the Soviet Political Adviser come to see me (I was for a time acting Political Adviser) to ask for the barbed wire to be removed. At the time we had a problem on the border between the British Sector and the DDR proper where the boundary ran down the middle of a road north of Staaken. Here the East Germans had for some reason dug an enormous hole on their side of the road that threatened to engulf any passing British patrol vehicle. The Soviet officer said this was an East German responsibility. I contested this on the usual lines. The meeting ended with no result but a couple of days later the hole was filled in by the East Germans and shortly after we removed the barbed wire from around the war memorial.

Under quadripartite agreements military personnel in uniform had freedom of movement throughout Berlin. Thus even after the construction of the Wall the Soviets could change guard at the Tiergarten memorial and take their month of guard duty at Spandau Prison every four months. The position of civilian members of the Allied military governments was different and there has been some criticism of the difference between US and British policies over movement through the East German controls in Friedrichstrasse/Checkpoint Charlie. US instructions were that their civilian officials should refuse to show identity documents to East Germans (e.g. the Lightner incident), whereas British civilian officials (such as me) were permitted to display (but not hand over) these. What lay behind this is that the vehicles of US civilian authorities in Berlin had license plates identifying the vehicle as Berlin-based and as such should have been permitted to pass straight through the controls. However, the cars of their British opposite numbers had plates similar to those used by the British Forces in Germany and occupants in civilian clothes could not be instantly identified as entitled to free movement throughout Berlin. Trivial, one might well think, but a difference that could and was exploited and misunderstood.

Later a not entirely dissimilar problem arose at Helmstedt (Checkpoint Alpha). The Soviets had difficulty in counting the number of soldiers in some US Army trucks because the height of the tailgate was such that a short Soviet officer could not see into the back of the truck. The British vehicles with lower tailgates did not encounter this problem. I like to think that some of the lack of automaticity and the insistence on a high level of political control over countermeasures or other responses in the event of Soviet or East German harassment may have very sensibly reflected the importance of distinguishing between an identity document and a true *casus belli*.

A few days after 13 August I saw a telegram from the British Chiefs of Staff to our military in Berlin and the Federal Republic. To the best of my recollection it underscored the importance of not being the first to use force. Although by then we were generally aware that Soviet forces around Berlin had been put on a high state of alert, the reasons for this instruction were clearly at least as much political as military. I had this instruction very much in mind when the episode described in the following paragraph took place.

It was a few days after 13 August. British Military Police used to patrol by Land Rover the border between the British Sector of Berlin and the DDR. North of Staaken the British Sector included an area of farmland bulging into the DDR known as the Eiskeller. Here the Military Police patrol drove over country tracks where the exact border was not clearly marked. Being both soldiers and police, from time to time by mistake they strayed into East Germany proper and this is what happened on this particular day. They were stopped by some East German police, arrested and taken away. I was telephoned by the officer in charge of the British forces in Berlin who told me what had taken place, saying also that he knew that our soldiers were being held in a building a few hundred yards inside the DDR. He asked me if he could he send in a fighting patrol to get his soldiers back. Having seen the clear instructions in the preceding paragraph, it was not difficult for me to tell him that he certainly must not do this. A few hours later, our military police were handed back, unharmed, at the Staaken border post and I may have stopped the outbreak of World War III! It may also have helped that I knew of occasions when British soldiers returning by S-Bahn after a night on the town had fallen asleep, failed to get off the train at the last station in the British Sector and had been stopped on arrival in the DDR, only to be returned shamefaced to us after a couple of hours detention in East Germany.

In the months following the construction of the Wall there was a lot of Western concern over Soviet action to carry out exercises in the three air corridors between the Federal Republic and Berlin that had been created by the immediately post-war quadripartite agreements. We continued to hold the Soviets responsible for avoiding trouble in the air corridors. There was contingency planning about what to do in the event of Soviet interference but this, as I recall, did not take place.

A final note

I was British ambassador in Warsaw when the communist regimes in Eastern Europe collapsed, the Wall came down and shortly afterwards the two Germanys became one again. Having been a junior diplomat when the Wall went up, I was and remain glad to see that something had gone right in that part of our world.

Sir Stephen Barrett

Above: A tour of the Wall in the Wedding district of Berlin, September 1961. *Below*: Checkpoint Charlie/Friedrich Strasse, December 1961 (Allied Museum Berlin/© US Army).

LIST OF PERSONS

Adenauer, Konrad, Federal German Chancellor, 1949-63
Amrehn, Franz K, Bürgermeister (Mayor) of West Berlin, 1955-63

Barrett, Stephen, Second Secretary (Deputy Political Adviser), BMG Berlin, 1959-62
Behrendt, Heinz, head, Office of Inter-German Trade, GDR Ministry of Foreign and Inter-German Trade, 1961
Brandt, Willy, *Regierender Bürgermeister,* West Berlin, 1957-66
Brentano, Heinrich von, Chairman CDU/CSU Group, *Bundestag,* 1949-55 and 1961-64

Caccia, Sir Harold, British Ambassador, Washington, 1956-61
Carstens, Karl, State-Secretary, 1960-66; Deputy Federal Minister of Foreign Affairs, 1961-66
Chauvel, Jean, French Ambassador, London, 1955-62
Clay, Gen Lucius D, Personal Representative of the US President, with rank of Ambassador, Berlin, 1961-62
Couve de Murville, Maurice, French Foreign Minister, 1958-68

Delacombe, Maj-Gen Rohan, GOC, Berlin (British Sector), 1959-62
Dibelius, Otto, Evangelical Bishop of Berlin-Brandenburg, 1945-66
Döpfner, Cardinal Julius, Roman Catholic Bishop of Berlin, 1957-61
Dowling Walter C, US Ambassador, Bonn, 1959-63
Duff, A. A, First Secretary, later Counsellor, British Embassy, Bonn, 1960-64
Durbrow, Elbridge, Deputy US Representative to the NATO Council of Ministers, Paris, 1961

Erhard, Professor Ludwig, Federal German Minister of Economic Affairs, 1949-63; Vice-Chancellor, 1957-63

Gaulle, Gen Charles de, French President, 1959-69
Grotewohl, Otto, Member, SED Politburo, 1946-64; GDR Prime Minister, 1949-64

Henderson, J. N, Assistant, Soviet Section, Northern Department, Foreign Office, 1959-63

Home, 14th Earl of, Secretary of State for Foreign Affairs, 1960-63

Johnson, Lyndon B, US Vice-President, 1961-63

Kennedy, John F, US President, 1961-63
Khrushchev, Nikita, First Secretary of Central Committee of the CPSU, 1953-64; Chairman of the Council of Ministers of the USSR, 1958-64
Kohler, Foy D, Assistant US Secretary of State (European Affairs), 1959-62
Kressmann, Willy K E, *Bürgermeister,* Berlin-Kreuzberg, 1949-62

Ledwidge, W Bernard, Political Adviser (Counsellor), British Political Branch, Berlin, 1956-61
Lemmer, Ernst, Federal German Minister for All-German Affairs, 1957-62
Leopold, Kurt, Head of the Berlin bureau of the Trust Office for Interzonal Trade, 1953-65

McDermott, Edward A, Deputy Director, US Office of Civil and Defense Mobilisation, the White House, 1960-61
McDermott, Geoffrey, Minister and Deputy Commandant, BMG Berlin, 1961-62
Macmillan, Harold, Prime Minister, 1957-63

Roberts, Sir Frank, British Ambassador, Moscow, 1960-63
Rumbold, Sir Horace, Minister, British Embassy, Paris, 1960-63
Rusk, D Dean, US Secretary of State, 1961-69

Shuckburgh, Sir Evelyn, DUS, FO, 1960-63
Smirnov, Andrei A, Ambassador, Bonn, 1957-66
Steel, Sir Christopher, British Ambassador, Bonn, 1957-63
Stikker, Dirk U, Netherlands Permanent Representative to NATO and to Council of OEEC, Paris, 1958-61

Ulbricht, Walter, General Secretary, SED, 1950-71; GDR Chairman of the Council of State, 1960-73

Watkinson, Harold A, Minister of Defence, 1959-62

ABBREVIATIONS

BAOR	British Army of the Rhine
BMG	British Military Government
CDU	*Christlich Demokratische Union*/Christian Democratic Union (FRG)
CSU	*Christlich-Soziale Union in Bayern*/Christian Social Union of Bavaria (FRG)
DDR	*Deutsche Demokratische Republik*/German Democratic Republic
DUS	Deputy Under-Secretary of State
FDP	*Freie Demokratische Partei*/Free Democratic Party (FRG)
FRG	Federal Republic of Germany
GDR	German Democratic Republic
GOC	General Officer Commanding
SACEUR	Supreme Allied Command Europe
SED	*Sozialistische Einheitspartei Deutschlands*/Socialist Unity Party of Germany (GDR)
SPD	*Sozialdemokratistische Partei Deutschlands*/German Social Democrat Party (FRG)
TTD	Temporary Travel Document
UKDEL	UK Delegation
UKMIS	UK Mission

Above: British troops in Berlin at the Brandenburg Gate, August 1961. *Below*: East German troops stand guard behind newly erected concrete barriers at the border between East and West Berlin, August 1961 (Allied Museum Berlin/© USIS).

LIST OF DOCUMENTS

1

Memorandum by the Earl of Home for the Cabinet[1]

C. (61)116 *Secret*   FOREIGN OFFICE, 26 July 1961

Berlin

Memorandum by the Secretary of State for Foreign Affairs

This paper (annexed) sets out some ideas on how we might approach the problem of Berlin in the coming weeks and what might be the basis for eventual negotiations with the Soviet Union. My colleagues may wish to consider this, together with memoranda (C. (61) 115 and C. (61) 118) circulated by the Minister of Defence in order to obtain a comprehensive view of the problem as a whole. It is not my intention at present to invite decisions upon the political aspects of the problem and I do not suggest that all the suggestions contained in the paper will necessarily stand up to further investigation.

2. I would summarise the tactical problem from the point of view of Her Majesty's Government as follows. Too much talk of military postures is undesirable because it is likely to frighten people rather than stiffen them and may easily start a rot among the neutrals. However, it is certainly right for the West to strengthen its hand against the eventuality of negotiations in an unprovocative and calm way. It is in this spirit that Mr Kennedy has presented his proposals.

3. On the other hand, too much talk of negotiation (for all that it is in principle fully accepted by the Americans) is embarrassing for them and risks encouraging charges that the British are 'soft' about Berlin. The best hope of reaching a negotiating position is through quiet diplomacy. The United States Secretary of State, Mr Rusk, agrees with this and I hope that the talks which the Foreign Ministers will have in Paris early in August will be kept as secret as possible so that they can be frank. Even so, they may not of course be very productive as it will be impossible to mention most of the ingredients of a possible successful negotiation with the Russians in front of the Germans, and the French will no doubt continue to make no effective contribution and to talk simply of standing firm. However, I would hope to find out at least in bilateral discussion with Mr Rusk how we can between us bring about negotiation to the best advantage.

H[ome]

---

[1] DBPO Ser. 3, Vol. 6, No. 232; CAB 129/106.

Annex

Berlin
The Problem

It is now clear that Mr Khrushchev intends to bring the Berlin question to a head this year. He will probably take the occasion of the XXIInd Party Congress on 17th October for an announcement of the signature of a separate peace treaty with East Germany, unless in the meantime something has occurred to deter him. The announcement would probably name a specific future date, probably a few days or weeks later, for convening a peace conference, although it is not impossible that it could say that the treaty is being signed forthwith. Mr Khrushchev has reserved for himself flexibility as to timing.

2. The declared Soviet doctrine is that a separate peace treaty with East Germany will provide for 'free city' status for West Berlin and cause Western rights in Berlin to lapse. Western troops may remain there, but their communications between West Germany and West Berlin will have to be negotiated with the sovereign East German Government. Mr Khrushchev has implied that, in default of such negotiations, these communications will be blocked and that any attempt to reopen them by force will be met by force. But here again there is uncertainty whether the communications would be impeded immediately or whether there would be a period of reasonableness on the part of the East Germans, followed by a slow squeeze designed to force us into closer and closer dealings with the *Deutsche Demokratische Republik* (DDR). Thus we cannot know when the physical interference with our rights and interests will occur.

3. But we assume that, unless by 17th October something has happened to deter Mr Khrushchev from signing a separate peace treaty, a physical challenge to our position in West Berlin will follow either at once or within a short time.

4. It is the general consensus of those who have seen Mr Khrushchev recently that he would still prefer a negotiated settlement if he can get one. The signature of a separate peace treaty with East Germany would certainly constitute a dramatic gesture of the sort which Mr Khrushchev probably wants to make for prestige reasons. It is not, however, the most satisfactory solution from his point of view. Apart from the grave danger of war which it may entail, it does not ensure Western recognition of the DDR and to some extent it would reduce Soviet control over events. It would be much better for Mr Khrushchev if he could force the West to negotiate with him a settlement which would have the effect of stabilising and legitimising the East German régime and weakening the Western position in Berlin.

5. It follows from this that Mr Khrushchev might be deterred from taking unilateral action in October if some real prospect of negotiation on terms which he would think satisfactory were opened up before that date.

6. Western opinion is moving fast in the direction of negotiation. The Federal German Chancellor, Dr Adenauer, himself has said publicly that he is convinced there will be negotiation this year. The American memorandum on Berlin handed to us by the State Department (which clearly has Presidential approval) proposes, as the second element in Western policy for the immediate future, 'an active diplomatic programme, including negotiations with the Soviet Union, designed to provide the Soviet leadership with an alternative course of action which does not endanger vital Western interests in Berlin'. The Soviet reaction to the last Western Notes has so far been mild and there is what seems to be an interest in negotiation in preference to unilateral action on the Soviet side.

What would we negotiate about?

7. Any negotiation on the subject of Germany and Berlin at the present time will be extremely tough and difficult, since Mr Khrushchev's aims are far-reaching, his position strong and his self-confidence very great. Leaving aside long-term Soviet objectives for Germany and any hope he may have of inflicting a humiliation on the Western Powers (see the memorandum on East/West Relations—C. (61) 97), it is probably fair to say that his minimum requirement will be a result which stabilises the DDR to a sufficient degree to lay the spectre of a unified, anti-Communist Germany. The weakness and instability of the DDR (so long as free West Berlin prevents its total isolation from the free world) is probably the main driving force behind Soviet insistence upon a change.

8. Putting the most charitable interpretation on Soviet motives, one can see their fear that an increasingly powerful and prosperous West Germany, clearly devoted to the concept of German reunification, may prove too powerful a magnet for all Germans and end by undermining the existence of the DDR unless the latter can be artificially stabilised and strengthened. If this is so, Mr Khrushchev's immediate objectives will be closely related to strengthening the DDR. They will be such things as forcing international recognition of the regime under the Chairman of the East German Council of State, Herr Ulbricht, and the pigeon-holing of German reunification as an aim; acceptance of the Eastern frontiers of Germany (Oder-Neisse line); elimination of the Berlin escape route for refugees; reduction of the worst effects of the Berlin 'example' on Eastern Germany and rendering the Western garrisons incapable of discharging their present task and loosening Berlin's ties with the Federal Republic. Behind these immediate objectives will lie the further longer-term hope of eliminating

the Western garrisons altogether, incorporating West Berlin in East Germany and loosening the Federal Republic's ties with the West, stopping the nuclear rearmament of Germany and, by breaking up the North Atlantic Alliance, bringing to an end American participation in Europe's defence.

9. Among these immediate Soviet objectives can be detected some things which are not wholly irreconcilable with Western policy. We could, for example, accept the stabilisation of Germany's eastern frontier on the Oder-Neisse line. Nor, in fact, do we really want German reunification, at least for the time being, though we cannot abandon the principle of self-determination for the Germans. The same is probably true of the rest of the North Atlantic Alliance, including the West Germans. German reunification now would upset what has been achieved in Western European integration since the war. We are not seeking to bring about the collapse of the East German regime through the departure of its most valuable citizens; on the contrary, we (and this includes the Federal Republic) are embarrassed by the greatly increased flow of refugees. If it were a question of a general stabilisation of the existing division in Europe, at least for a period of years, we should presumably have no reason to object; indeed, given the strength of the Soviet position on the ground we should probably consider ourselves lucky to obtain it. Unpleasant though it would be to have to bolster up a Communist dictatorship like that of Herr Ulbricht, it is not necessarily the case that in the long run a peace treaty with that regime would be detrimental to freedom in Germany. For the East German regime will not reach the end of its troubles merely by acquiring a degree of international recognition, nor even by reducing the nuisance of Berlin. It is at least arguable that the influence of the 47 million West Germans could be brought to bear more effectively on the 17 million East Germans if the Federal Government would pursue a different policy and be prepared to enter into closer relationships with the East German regime. They have hitherto shown remarkable lack of courage in this respect.

10. In other words, it seems not inconceivable that we could build a negotiating policy on the broad principle of stabilisation for a period of years, say for the next five years, and that we could reach a practical deal with Mr Khrushchev on this basis without either side being compelled to abandon any really crucial position. It must be recognised that under any such deal the West would have necessarily abandoned a certain number of principles which have hitherto been strongly held. Such a policy would mean placing the Berlin problem in a wider frame and attempting a general—if provisional—stabilisation of the German situation. Possible elements out of which such a deal might be constructed are as follows:

(*a*) We should accept the decision of the Soviets and their friends to sign a peace treaty with East Germany and be willing to deal with the DDR as the de facto authority in East Germany.

(*b*) We need not ourselves sign a peace treaty with East Germany or recognise it de jure. It would probably be necessary, however, for the Federal Government to abandon the 'Hallstein' doctrine whereby they refuse diplomatic relations with any country which enters into similar relations with the DDR. The result of this will be a great increase of East German diplomatic activity throughout the world. A longer term result might be a move for the admission of both Germanys into the United Nations.

(*c*) We might urge the Federal Government to consider the possibility of establishing contacts with East Germany which would go some way in the direction of the confederal relationship between the two Germanys which the Russians urge.

(*d*) We could recognise the overall frontiers of Germany (Oder-Neisse line).

(*e*) Our conditions for all this would be a guarantee by the Russians that the present status of West Berlin would be preserved (i.e., no free city in the Russian sense and no Russian troops) and that Western access to West Berlin, both civilian and military, would be fully and freely maintained by their clients, the DDR authorities. We would not insist on regarding the DDR personnel as agents of the Russians; we would deal with them on their own merits as de facto German authorities; but the Russians would have undertaken a contractual obligation towards us to see that our access was not interfered with and we would seek redress of grievances from them and not from the DDR Government. We would claim that our existing rights remained valid at the same time, but we need not insist on their admitting it.

(*f*) The Russians would not give such guarantees regarding the behaviour of *their* German allies without asking us for guarantees about the behaviour of ours. We might be able to contemplate agreements on the following points:

(i) That there will be no manufacture or possession of nuclear weapons by Germans in any part of Germany during the lifetime of the arrangement.

(ii) That no missiles or nuclear weapons will be brought within X miles of the demarcation line or into Berlin.

(iii) That certain activities of a propagandist nature will not take place in any part of Berlin. We might admit United Nations or neutral (but not Russian) observers into West Berlin to confirm that these undertakings were being observed (with reciprocal arrangements for East Berlin).

(iv) That West Berlin might offer space and accommodation on an extraterritorial basis to certain organs of the United Nations. This might both make it easier for the Russians to justify granting a guarantee of access and offer them some assurance of responsible behaviour in West Berlin. There might possibly be a similar arrangement in East Berlin.

(v) It is for consideration whether there is any means of limiting the flow of refugees which would be tolerable from the Western and from the humane point of view. At present the refugees are being flown out of West Berlin in allied aircraft as if they were allied traffic. This is legally tenable but seems to be stretching our rights rather far; but it is apparently hallowed by usage and would be very difficult to end. The very fact of a settlement having been reached would tend to reduce the flow.

(g) It is worth examining whether, in this connection, some kind of nuclear disengagement on a wider basis could be proposed and whether plans for an area of limitation of armaments and armed forces or the prevention of surprise attack, with mutual air inspection of both sides of the line, might not also be revived.

(h) A non-aggression agreement between the North Atlantic Alliance and the Warsaw Pact, though fairly meaningless, might be added for good measure.

How to bring about negotiation

11. It must not be supposed that we shall have an easy task in persuading our allies that a deal of this kind is even desirable and our most difficult problem in the coming weeks will be to decide how and when it is safe even to hint to them that we are thinking along these lines. Nor have we any idea whether this sort of solution would meet Mr Khrushchev's demands, though the most recent indications from Moscow suggest that it might. Clearly it would be very wrong to let him have sight of any of the concessions which are involved in this plan in advance of real negotiation.

12. Our aims for the time being must therefore be limited:

(a) To ensuring that the door is left open to negotiation and Mr Khrushchev given no excuse for premature unilateral action before the German elections.

(b) To ensuring that the West is ready by the end of September with an agreed proposal for negotiations or for a summit meeting. We shall have to pursue this aim with great discretion.

(c) To keeping up a certain pressure on Mr Khrushchev and strengthening our hand for eventual negotiations by maintaining a posture of unity and strength in the Alliance.

13. The latest American memorandum describes in acceptable terms the line to be pursued in the immediate future. It suggests:

(a) Informal and quiet probing of the Soviet position through the diplomatic channel in Moscow 'to warn of possible consequences of that position in terms of Allied military build-up, and to take advantage of any opportunities which might appear to move towards a subsequent understanding on an arrangement which might be acceptable'.

(*b*) Exploration of opportunities for Western political initiatives 'at an appropriate time'—depending of course partly on Soviet moves and partly on the timetable of the German elections.

The United Nations and public opinion

14. If it becomes evident that no serious negotiation can be undertaken, or if serious negotiation appears about to break down, we shall have to consider methods of establishing a favourable position with public opinion and with the United Nations. It may indeed be necessary to bring the United Nations in at an earlier stage. It has been suggested, for example, that the United States Government would want to associate the United Nations in some way with any offer of negotiation. There is also the certainty that if the Berlin crisis began to look really dangerous, neutral governments would not be lacking to bring it before the United Nations as a threat to the peace.

15. United Nations intervention would be bound to result in fuller international recognition of the DDR and would involve a need for more flexibility by the Federal German Government than they have hitherto shown. The tendency would be for the United Nations to put the preservation of world peace above the interests of the West Berliners and above Allied rights in Berlin and there would be a danger of the United Nations endorsing situations unacceptable to the West and condemning any Western counter action.

16. On the other hand, a properly timed and directed Western initiative in the United Nations might be effective in getting world public opinion on our side. The Russians are on balance likely to take considerable account of world public opinion as expressed in the United Nations, provided that what they regard as vital Soviet interests are satisfied. Moreover, it might well be easier to persuade the West German Government to accept a compromise German settlement if this originated in the United Nations and was acquiesced in rather than promoted by the Western Powers.

17. We must therefore assume that, unless a settlement is reached with the Soviet Union before the Berlin crisis becomes acute, the United Nations will become involved in one way or another and may find ourselves obliged to consider taking an initiative ourselves at the appropriate moment.

18. Concurrently with action in the United Nations we might want to put forward alternative 'solutions' of the Berlin problem, not because we

expected them to be accepted but in order to show a reasonable and constructive attitude. Such arguments might include:

(*a*) A free city of *all* Berlin, with free access from East and West and a corridor, under United Nations guarantee.

(*b*) A plebiscite in all Berlin.

(*c*) Transfer of the United Nations Headquarters to Berlin, and establishment of a United Nations city.

Devices such as the Brandt plan for a conference of the ex-enemies of Germany should also be borne in mind.

Letter from Mr Ledwidge (BMG Berlin) to Mr Duff (Bonn)[1]

Confidential   BERLIN, 27 July 1961

Michael Rose sent me under cover of compliments slip (1821) of July 19 a copy of your minute suggesting some study of the possible effects of a continuation of the present high refugee flow on East German and, more particularly, Soviet policy on the Berlin and German questions.

2. Our comment on questions as broad as those raised in your minute must necessarily be speculative. With this proviso, we should say that the increased refugee flow and the general situation in East Germany are weak points in the communist position which should make the Russians rather more willing to moderate their demands in the hope of achieving a negotiated settlement. But it is hard to weigh these factors against other weighty considerations such as the Russian estimate of Western military strength and willingness to use it. Finally, we think serious trouble in East Germany improbable but not impossible. The Russians would certainly crush any physical resistance, unless the West intervened physically. In the following paragraphs we develop these ideas.

3. The continuing drain of refugees is undoubtedly having an increasingly serious effect on the East German economy. One illustration of its cumulative effect is that we now see more refugees who had held positions of some responsibility and decided to come out because their jobs had become impossible to perform as a result of defections further down the line. The effect of the refugee flow on the economy is relative to the magnitude of the tasks which the economy is set. It must be seen against a background of ambitious plans for swift industrial expansion and at the same time, for sweeping social change. We do not think there is any question of a dramatic breakdown in the East German economy, and doubt whether it is possible to establish a particular estimated point beyond which a further increase in the refugee flow would produce economic disaster. The Russians need not worry about that. Their difficulty is rather that, so long as the flow continues, the DDR will never really 'get off the ground' either economically or politically, and will continue to present a most unpleasing picture to the world at large. It will be difficult to make the DDR look much better even by concluding a separate peace treaty with it. The increased flow is clearly a disgrace to the Russian and German communists; and western publicity has recently rubbed this in effectively.

---

[1] DBPO Ser. 3, Vol. 6, No. 253; CG 1018/22.

4. At this point we might mention the revival here of the perennial rumour that the Russians are tired of Ulbricht and have decided to replace him. The story now being canvassed in left-wing SPD circles in West Berlin is that Grotewohl is not really so ill as reports make out and that he is being groomed by the Russians to take over from Ulbricht before the end of the year. Of course we do not believe this; but we can believe that Ulbricht's recent performance has disappointed the Russians

5. The East Germans are trying to cut down the refugee flow both by a vigorous propaganda campaign designed to reassure the population about the consequences of a separate peace treaty and by sharper controls on access from the Zone to East Berlin. But we doubt whether they will have much success. At any rate let us assume for the purposes of this letter that in the coming months a high refugee rate continues. We think that the difficulties in the DDR would then lead Ulbricht to press even more strongly for a radical solution of the problem on the lines of the separate peace treaty, But how will Khrushchev feel? We are not competent here to express an authoritative opinion on Soviet aims and tactics. It does seem to us, however, a better than even chance that the current deterioration of the situation in East Germany, with its attendant risks of popular demonstrations if the safety-valve were suddenly closed, would tend to increase the attractiveness in Russian eyes of a solution negotiated with the West—even an interim solution—as against a separate peace treaty which would commit the Soviet Government to a dangerous effort to impose a Berlin solution unilaterally upon the Western Powers. If it were to prove impossible for the Russians, even by stretching a few points, to achieve an agreement with the West which they could describe as satisfactory, they might then be encouraged by their difficulties in East Germany to sign a separate peace treaty revised and modified so as to minimise the chance of its leading to a head-on clash with the West.

6. Even if it does come to a separate treaty, we are inclined to think that some refugees will still be allowed to get through. Given the risks of an '*Ausbruch*', the Russians (and East Germans) may think it prudent merely to close the safety valve half or three quarters of the way.

7. Since this is a speculative exercise, let us end on a flesh-creeping note. We agree with the assumptions in paragraph 3 of your minute that there is little likelihood of any serious trouble in East Germany before the conclusion of a separate peace treaty and that any such trouble arising afterwards would be unlikely to be of an organised nature and would be dealt with summarily by the Soviet and East German forces. But it is worth reminding ourselves that the disturbances of 1953 took us almost completely by surprise, and that we also underestimated the extent to which the DDR regime was shaken by events in Poland and Hungary in

1956. Many refugees now speak quite spontaneously of the similarity of the atmosphere in the East Zone to-day to that in 1956 and even 1953. Remote as the contingency may be, therefore, we ought not completely to rule out the possibility that if the West Stands firm the Russians may be confronted with something like a repetition of what happened in Poland in 1956; that is to say the sudden emergence in East Germany of a communist government which, while vowing loyalty to Moscow, wanted to adapt its policy on Berlin and Germany to some extent to the wishes of the majority of the population. Such a situation, if mishandled, could of course turn into a second Hungary. Then the Russians and the West would have to decide what to do about it.

W. B. J. LEDWIDGE

Telegram from the Foreign Office to Maj-Gen Delacombe
(BMG Berlin)[1]

Tel. No. 132 *Priority Secret*   FOREIGN OFFICE, 10 August 1961
                                                           D. 8.20 p.m.

Repeated for information to Bonn.

The growth in the numbers of refugees who are escaping from East
Germany is causing us some concern since there is an obvious danger that
East German attempts to stop them may complicate the Berlin problem
still further and possibly even precipitate a crisis.

2. We should be grateful if you would keep us closely informed about
this matter and in particular if you would let us have your assessment of
the effect of this exodus on the DDR and your opinion whether there is
any likelihood that the flow may fall off of its own accord before very
long.

---

[1] DBPO Ser. 3 Vol. 6 No. 256; CG 1821/18.

Telegram from Maj-Gen Delacombe (BMG Berlin) to the Foreign Office[1]

Tel. No. 270 *Immediate Confidential*   BERLIN, 12 August 1961
D. 7.45 p.m.
R. 8.10 p.m.

Repeated for information to Bonn, Washington and Saving to Paris, Moscow and UKDEL NATO.

Your telegram No. 132 (not to all) and Bonn telegram No. 45 to me: East German Refugees.

The refugee flow through Berlin continues to grow, totaling 12,210 registrations last week, some 2,000 more than the previous week. At this rate August will much exceed the July total of just over 30,000. While refugees continue to come out because they expect a better life in West Germany, the main immediate motive for the increased flow is undoubtedly the fear that the escape route may shortly be closed.

2. The most significant variation in the composition of the increased flow is the greater proportion (20-25%) of *Grenzgaenger* and their dependents. Otherwise the composition remains stable, reflecting the normal seasonal fluctuations, e.g. more children and teachers come out during the holiday. One deviation is that refugees in the age group 18 to 25 have dropped from 30% in June to 25% in July, which reflects the particular attention paid by police to this category.

3. Since mid-July the DDR authorities have imposed stricter police controls, particularly on the railways, where travellers are now often checked at their point of departure as well as en route or on arrival at a station near Berlin. The numbers removed from trains for questioning, sending back or other measures has increased; yet very many get through, which demonstrates the difficulty of control during the holiday season and shows that some policemen are turning a blind eye. In the last month a propaganda campaign of great virulence has been launched against those inciting or assisting refugees (the so-called 'traffic in human beings'), and there have been 'show trials' in East Germany with heavy sentences. The number of refugees travelling with inter-zonal passes, i.e. with official permission to visit West Germany, dropped both absolutely and relatively in July, when the proportion of those with such passes was lower than at

---

[1] DBPO Ser. 3, Vol. 6, No. 257; CG 1821/8.

any time since 1953.

4. The increased refugee flow is determined not so much by the imminence of a peace treaty per se (this has indeed somewhat receded with the announcement of a bloc Foreign Ministers meeting in late Autumn) as by the popular fear that the escape route will be closed even earlier. The DDR authorities cannot credibly remove this fear by soothing statements particularly in the fact of their own *Menschenhandel* propaganda. But definite news that East/West negotiations were to take place before a peace treaty probably would ease this fear and cause the flow to decrease, as it did during past periods of negotiation.

5. The other way of checking the flow is by much stricter controls. As to these, it seems possible that Khrushchev's and Ulbricht's assessment of the dangers of an explosion if the door were shut may be at variance and that Ulbricht may have been told in Moscow that he must not take the risk of imposing a complete closure. In that event the (unspecified) further measures foreshadowed by the Volkskammer meeting on August 11 may turn out to be only a more concentrated dose of the mixture as before. It seems that the main effort may be directed against movement from the Soviet Zone to Berlin. Movement between East and West Berlin is slightly riskier than it was but still pretty free. Sharper controls on East Berliners would be likely to cause an immediate increase in the total flow, as Brandt has warned us. It is hard to explain the Volkskammer performance unless appreciably more stringent controls follow. So far this has not happened. The immediate effect has merely been to stimulate a further rush of refugees. If no further measures at all are taken in the next few days, it would suggest that the Russians have had second thoughts since the Volkskammer meeting was convened.

6. Any stringently increased controls are likely to increase the exasperation of the East German people, the vast majority of whom are deeply disturbed by the implications of the 'peace treaty' policy. There have already been cases of incitement to violence against would-be refugees or those who speak well of conditions in West Germany, and this may also lead to counter-violence and local disturbances. We doubt, however, whether more than minor local disturbances are likely at any rate so long as there is some possibility (albeit restricted) of escape. The presence of Soviet troops will continue to make a general uprising highly unlikely. Organized 'non-cooperation' on a country-wide basis can we think be ruled out, unless incited from outside. The régime is extremely sensitive to any signs of 'non-cooperation' in individual factories. 'Go-slow' or deliberately obstructive methods of work among forcibly collectivised farmers are, however, already a problem to the régime, and contribute to the poor state of East German agriculture this year.

7. To sum up, the refugee flow is inflicting increasing political and economic damage on the DDR, though there is no question of sudden, dramatic breakdown. The Russians are probably more impressed by the dangers of disturbances if the escape route is completely cut than by the current damage to the DDR. It is therefore likely that refugees will continue to come out, with the East German authorities confining their efforts to an attempt to hold the position and if possible reverse the strong upward trend. The end of the school holidays may help to reduce numbers a little but there is no prospect of the flow declining much of its own accord in present circumstances. Meanwhile Khrushchev may expect the pressure to be somewhat eased by improved prospects for East/West negotiations. We would not consider that the refugee flow will in itself precipitate an acute crisis. Rather we should say that the state of affairs within East Germany increases for Khrushchev the attractiveness of some agreement with the Western Powers as against a unilaterally imposed 'settlement' of the German problem.

5

Telegram from Maj-Gen Delacombe (BMG Berlin) to the Foreign Office[1]

Tel. No. 271 *Emergency Confidential*   BERLIN, 13 August 1961
                                                          D. 8.47.a.m.
                                                          R. 8.55 a.m.

Repeated for information to Foreign Office, Washington, Paris, UKMIS New York, HQRAF Germany, UKDEL NATO, Moscow, HQ BAOR and Saving to Prague and Warsaw.

Berlin Situation.

In early hours of August 13, East German Radio announced a series of measures by DDR Government imposing much stricter controls on access of East Germans including East Berliners to West Berlin. They are described as 'controls usual at state frontiers'.

2. Announcement was prefaced by a statement by Warsaw Pact Powers proclaiming need, in absence of a peace settlement with Germany, for immediate action to protect socialist camp, and above all, DDR itself, against subversion directed from West Berlin. Statement calls on DDR Government to take appropriate measures and blames Western powers and, above all, Federal Republic for their necessity. Measures taken are to be valid until a peace treaty is signed.

3. Following are salient points in new measures:

(i) DDR citizens, including East Berliners, will in future need a special permit to visit West Berlin;

(ii) they are no longer permitted to work in West Berlin;

(iii) S-bahn and U-bahn traffic will be greatly reduced and subjected to much stricter controls;

(iv) number of sector crossing-points for cars and pedestrians will be much reduced.

4. An announcement by DDR Ministry of Interior states that there will be no (repeat no) change in arrangements governing access of Western occupation forces to East Berlin. Regulations on access to East Berlin of West Berliners, West Germans and foreigners are also unchanged, but 'revanchists' will not be admitted.

5. It is also announced that arrangements governing traffic of goods and persons between West Berlin and West Germany will remain

---

[1] DBPO Ser. 3, Vol. 6, No. 258; CG 10113/11.

unchanged.

6. New controls began to take effect during the night. Police reinforcements have moved to main sector crossing points and many wiring parties are at work. S-bahn traffic is much below normal.

7. Main target of new controls is clearly the refugee stream. *Grenzgaenger* are a secondary target. If the controls are strictly enforced they should reduce the refugee stream to a trickle, we shall report as soon as effects are visible.

6

Telegram from Maj-Gen Delacombe (BMG Berlin) to the Foreign Office [1]

Tel. No. 272 *Immediate Confidential*   BERLIN, 13 August 1961
D. 3.40 p.m.
R. 3.50 p.m.

Repeated for information to Foreign Office, Washington, Paris, UKDEL NATO, HQ BAOR, HQ RAF Germany, Moscow, UKMIS New York and Saving to Prague and Warsaw.

My immediately preceding telegram: Berlin Situation.

The three Commandants met with the governing Mayor and Mayor this morning to hear views of West Berlin authorities. Brandt began by saying that it was difficult to predict the reaction of East Germans to the DDR measures, which he said would be regarded as setting up a concentration camp fence across the city. It could not be ruled out that the DDR population would be driven to acts of desperation. He mentioned the possibility of incidents tonight or tomorrow morning (i.e. when popular reaction had time to develop and when *Grenzgaenger* might attempt to cross into West Berlin). The refugee flow had been sharply reduced: only 150 had come out so far today and these had escaped by coming through ruins etc. For their part the Senate were conscious of the need to weigh carefully any public statements and would avoid saying anything that might inflame West Berlin or DDR population. There would be a meeting of the West Berlin House of Representatives this evening at which he would report on the situation. They would welcome the attendance of the Commandants at this.

2. Brandt thought it was unnecessary to mobilize the police, who had already been alerted. Any measures necessary would be taken to ensure that West Berliners did not cause any incidents on the sector borders or on S-Bahn stations.

3. In the view of the Senate the gravity of the situation warranted high level representations to the Soviets. The fact that the DDR measures were introduced following statement issued by Warsaw Pact governments might make it appropriate for the Western Ambassadors in Moscow to take action. But they also thought that the Commandants should take some action in Berlin, and that consideration should be given in Bonn to

---

[1] DBPO Ser. 3, Vol. 6, No. 259; CG 10113/12.

economic counter-measures. He asked that the Commandants should convey these views to their Higher Authorities. He did not mention restricting East German travel to Western countries.

4. Report on Commandants meeting and recommendations follow.

7

Telegram from Supreme Allied Command Europe (NATO)[1]

SACEUR Tel. SH29658 *Immediate Confidential*   14 August 1961

Following is summary of Berlin situation as of 131700Z Aug received from NATO Source.

1. No restrictions currently applied to autobahn, rail or air corridor travel to and from Berlin, except those imposed on East German citizens attempting to reach West Berlin.

2. No incidents reported in air corridors or on autobahns.

3. Allied military liaison mission tours still free to travel without other than usual restrictions.

4. One mission reports that the Soviet 19th Motorized Rifle Division, combined with 10th Guards Tank Division and possibly the 6th Motorized Rifle Division moved out early this morning and moved into positions around Berlin. Elements of the 1st East German Army Motorized Rifle Division moved out from Potsdam and are presently unlocated. Soviet units deployed and move off of the autobahn deploying units into small outposts and roundblocks composed of three or four tanks, an armoured personnel carrier and several troops. These out-posts were established about three to four kilometers apart, and appear completely to ring Berlin. Deployment of forces as follows:

A. Soviet 19th Motorized Rifle Division north and west of Berlin.

B. 10th Guards Tank Division south of Berlin.

C. 6th Motorized Rifle Division possibly east of Berlin completing ring around Berlin.

Local consensus that mission of deployed Soviet forces around Berlin is to back up VOPOS (Peoples Police) and Security Alert Police in cutting of refugee flow and to forestall civilian disturbances.

5. In East Berlin, East German Border Security Police, VOPOS Security Alert Police and District Alert Police, backed up by some unidentified East German army personnel and tanks have effectively sealed the sector to sector borders. Barbed wire barricades have been erected at most crossing points and armed police are at all points. The streets are heavily patrolled. Thirteen (13) of the one hundred twenty (120) Sector to Sector border crossing points remain open for controlled flow of West Berliners and foreigners travelling to and from East Berlin. Very limited S-Bahn (railway) service exists between West Berlin and East

---

[1] DBPO Ser. 3, Vol. 6, No. 263; CG 10113/21.

Berlin.

6. Controls on the borders are extremely effective, as indicated by the fact that only less than 100 (estimated) refugees have crossed the border since 130500Z. Of this small number, several swam canals and one automobile ran to concertina wire barricade.

7. Incidents have been restricted to large curious crowd of West Berliners gathered in vicinity of the Soviet War Memorial in front of the Brandenburg Gate. Crowd is under complete control. One or two reports have been received of attempts to tear down wire barricades at crossing points but news reports of East Germans bayonetting civilian personnel are unconfirmed. West Berlin police remain on alert status. Mayor Brandt considered that possibility exists for an organized assembly of West Berlin citizens tonight following session of Senate. Possibility of incidents or demonstrations exists in the event a large crowd does gather.

8. Brandt addressed the Senate tonight with the Commandants and Deputies in attendance.

9. In conclusion, the situation in Berlin as of 1700Z 13th Aug is quiet, under control and with few incidents thus far. Border is effectively sealed off the refugee flow.

10. Press reports have been largely factual, but tend toward sensationalism.

Sources state difficulty in establishing identity of Soviet units moving to encircle Berlin has led to several conflicting reports during the day. Unit dispositions reported in para four (4) is still subject to confirmation but fact of encirclement at least for purposes stated is established.

Principal chances for incidents during the night 13-14 Aug and early 14 appear to lie in possibility of:

A. Crowds getting out of control before they can be finally dispersed for the night.

B. 'Borders crossers' creating incidents on morning of 14 August at time they would normally cross sector border into West Berlin to go to the jobs now denied them by E.G. decree.

8

Telegram from Sir C. Steel (Bonn) to the Foreign Office[1]

Tel. No. 781 *Immediate Secret*   BONN, 14 August 1961
                                                   D. 5.00 p.m.
                                                   R. 5.15 p.m.

Repeated for information to Washington, Paris, UKDEL NATO and Moscow.

My telegram No. 777.
    I have been greatly struck by the insistence of both Carstens in Paris and Brentano this morning that Soviet and East German proceedings in Berlin were essentially part of their long term designs on Berlin (which means our position there) and not to be ascribed to compulsions of any kind, either internally to Russian, or from China, or finally from situation in East Germany. This puzzled me in Paris but Brentano's line this morning was so at variance with the obvious facts of the situation that I think there is another explanation. By this, I mean that Khrushchev so clearly wishes to bring us to the conference table while the situation is fluid and not to risk (any more than we want to risk) anything like a dangerous fait accompli or showdown that he would not have started this manoeuvre except under pressure. Despite the bold face put on it by Communist propaganda it is the worst wicket from his point of view and the care with which other Western interests have been treated, i.e. even access to East Berlin, seems to me significant. The only explanation which fits the case is that the Germans are conscious of Western disinterest in reunification of rather our determination not to make this casus belli. Kohler told Carstens in Paris very clearly that we should not so treat it and it was after this that he departed so mysteriously for Cadenabbia. As you will see, both Dowling and I challenged Brentano's interpretation of Soviet motives, although curiously our French colleague seemed to support him. The matter was left without the issue having been seriously joined.
    2. I think this is as well since the Federal Government are not really interested in reunification and their attitude is all politics. But in the difficult business of framing Allied policy over the coming weeks, I think we should bear this angle in mind, I must say that I personally have always wondered that the East Germans have waited so long to seal this boundary.

---

[1] DBPO Ser. 3, Vol. 6, No. 268; CG 10113/18.

I think that hitherto it has been the fear of West German and Allied sanctions which stopped them doing so (as last winter) but the cumulative defections of the past month have forced them to action. I should think that in any settlement it would be almost impossible for us to re-establish a situation where East Germans are more or less free to leave the Communist world at will. We ought really, therefore, to get together with the Americans as soon as possible—albeit cautiously—to ensure that they, no more than we, regard this as the issue on which we break. The operation looks like being extremely delicate, and for this reason, the recommendation in my telegram No. 775 that we ought to use this as a peg for a negotiation seems to me a long way the best solution. At all costs we must avoid any kind of dispute in the Allied ranks at this time as to what we would not fight for.

9

Telegram from the Earl of Home to Sir C. Steel (Bonn)[1]

Tel. No. 1555 *Immediate Secret*   FOREIGN OFFICE, 14 August 1961
D. 8.10 p.m.

Repeated for information to Berlin [Immediate], Paris [Immediate], Washington [Emergency], UKDEL NATO, Moscow, HQ BAOR, HQ RAF Germany.

Your telegram No. 777 (paragraph 2) [of August 14: Berlin].

As you know I agree that we must react strongly to these East German measures but I have serious doubts about the wisdom of suspending TTDs.

2. In the first place we have always taken the view that counter measures should be taken if there was interference with access to Berlin or with the freedom of movement throughout Berlin for inhabitants of West Berlin. Though we have protested at Soviet or East German efforts to restrict the freedom of movement of East Berliners we have never actually tried to stop them and I do not think that we should do so in this case since our interests are not directly involved.

3. An even stronger reason for not imposing a ban on TTDs is that such a measure would be most unlikely to produce the desired result. When we did so last year there was always a good chance that the East Germans were only testing out reactions and that if these were firm enough they would lift their restrictions on freedom of movement in Berlin. In the event they did so. The present case is quite different. Since they are acting out of desperation there seems to be no hope whatever of their lifting the restrictions and the ban on TTDs would thus be not provisional but permanent. This would amount in fact to a move towards an economic blockade, which in present circumstances is neither necessary nor desirable. Moreover it would put Her Majesty's Government in a very difficult situation since whatever the Germans may do to restrict travel, the ban on TTDs would inevitably have a much more severe effect on trade between this country and East Germany than on interzonal trade. In these circumstances it would not be long before parliamentary pressure forced us to ask for exceptions which would greatly diminish the value of the whole operation. I expect that this would also be true of several other members of NATO. Finally there is a danger that the East Germans would consider any measures taken by the Federal Government as a violation of

---

[1] DBPO Ser. 3 Vol. 6 No. 269; CG 10113/16.

the Leopold Behrendt agreement and use this as a justification for closing the Eastern Sector off completely and interfering with civilian traffic to Berlin. This would lead to a further increase in tension which we are all agreed should be avoided.

4. My opinion is therefore that the suspension of TTDs should be reserved as a counter to actions which have a direct effect on our interests, individual or collective, and not simply as a demonstration of disapproval at the illegal actions of the East German authorities.

10

Telegram from the Earl of Home to Sir H. Caccia (Washington)[1]

Tel. No. 5493 *Emergency Secret*   FOREIGN OFFICE, 14 August 1961
D. 9.20 p.m.

Repeated for information to: Paris, Bonn, Moscow, Berlin, UKMIS New York and Saving to UKDEL NATO.

Your telegram No. 1914 (of August 14): Berlin
Following from Shuckburgh.

I understand from the French that you have a meeting of the Ambassadorial Group this evening. Following thoughts, which have not been seen by the Secretary of State, are sent for your guidance. You should not commit the Secretary of State, particularly on the question of the timing of any meetings with the Russians, but should try to explore the views of your colleagues.

2. The East German restrictions clearly create a potentially dangerous situation. It is satisfactory that the Americans are concerned, as we are, that nothing should be said or done by the West to increase the tension or to stimulate uprising in East Germany. The statements so far made by Dr Adenauer and Herr Brandt seem satisfactory from this point of view.

3. For reasons given in my telegram No. 1555 to Bonn, we are very doubtful about the appropriateness of applying a provisional suspension of TTDs as suggested by Brentano (Bonn telegram No. 777).

4. The choices now confronting us are well set out in Sir C. Steel's telegram No. 775. Certainly we should make a formal protest in Moscow and I assume that the Ambassadorial Group will be drafting this. I understand that the Quai d'Orsay have prepared a draft which they are showing to General de Gaulle this evening. The question is whether these Notes should be confined to formal protest or whether they should include a demand for discussion with the Soviet Government on the grounds of the dangerous tensions created by the East Germans' action. Consideration should also be given to the question of taking up in the Notes some of the points on which the Soviet Government's latest Note shows them to be sensitive; in particular freedom of choice for the Germans and the alleged aggressions of the Federal Government. On the first point, should we now propose a plebiscite?

---

[1] DBPO Ser. 3 Vol. 6 No. 270; CG 10113/14.

5. A proposal for discussions on the immediate situation arising from the DDR travel restrictions would no doubt be more advantageous for us than negotiation along the lines hitherto proposed by Khrushchev. The Communists are in an exposed position through being compelled to put barbed wire round their own populations and from the public relations point of view this is as good an issue as we are likely to find for proposing discussions. But the Russians would no doubt reply that the reason for the trouble lay in the absence of a treaty of peace and that in any case the measures taken by the DDR authorities were an internal matter. Thus if we got negotiations going by this means we should still find it very difficult to avoid discussion of the substance of the Berlin problem as a whole, for which of course we are not ready before September 17. Timing therefore seems to be the main objection to this idea. It would not be logical to claim that there was an emergency situation requiring consultation between the Four Powers and then to suggest that these consultations should be delayed for six weeks or so.

6. We do not know to what extent, if at all, President Kennedy's thoughts about the timing of an announcement of willingness to negotiate had been affected by the very negative response which Mr Rusk received from General de Gaulle. Nor do we know what his present intentions are about possible soundings through the diplomatic channel in Moscow. Anything you can discover about this would be very valuable. One point on which it might be interesting to probe Mr Khrushchev is whether the fact that events have forced him to agree to the DDR dealing with the refugee problem through restrictions on their side of the border has altered his intentions about dealing with the problem of access to West Berlin, e.g. by retaining it in his own hands as something with which he could do a bargain with the West. This is an idea which you might try out on the Americans alone.

7. We have looked again at the alternative idea mentioned by Sir C. Steel of launching an appeal to the United Nations and we still think that it has serious dangers and should be avoided until a moment arrives at which it seems inevitable that somebody else is going to bring the United Nations in.

11

Telegram from Sir C. Steel (Bonn) to the Foreign Office[1]

Tel. No. 785 *Immediate Secret*   BONN, 15 August 1961
D. 11.54 a.m.
R. 12.08 a.m.

Repeated for information Immediate to Washington and to Paris, Moscow, UKDEL NATO, HQ BAOR and HQ RAF (Germany).

Berlin.
Your telegram No. 1555: Berlin (TTDs).

I was aware when we saw Brentano that you were likely to have doubts about TTDs and I was careful to elicit undertakings from him that any restrictions on our side would be matched by the Germans. On the other hand, I must say that I think we shall be in difficulties if we take no steps whatsoever of a concrete character and confine ourselves to protests. In calling for restraint, the Federal Government are going to have a hard time with the Berliners, and Adenauer has already announced that there will be counter-measures. It would not be a pretty situation if it were to come out that the allies were leaving the Federal Government out on a limb, thanks to the usual British indecision. Sebastian Haffner (*Observer* correspondent in Berlin) has a poisonous article in *Die Welt* this morning attacking us and the Americans for being relieved that our own position in Berlin is not at issue and it is only the E. Germans and E. Berliners who are suffering.

2. I can quite see the logic of your contention that when we imposed these restrictions last year it was in answer to restrictions on West Berliners entering East Berlin, but of course although the main emphasis is now on East Berliners entering West Berlin full control of West Berliners has now been reintroduced and the 'revanchists' are to be excluded. This will immediately be cited by the Germans and indeed Brentano said yesterday that a revanchist could mean any citizen of the Federal Republic.

3. I can also see the advantages of having a further weapon in reserve for other occasions but despite these I consider that we shall have to use this one now. To begin with, we still have a lot of other economic sanctions available supposing there is any kind of interruption of access to West Berlin. The most important of these would clearly be the Federal Government's control of trade with the DDR, but we have others.

---

[1] DBPO Ser. 3 Vol. 6, No. 272; CG 10113/16.

Moreover, there is an argument on the other side. If, as now seems inevitable, we are soon involved in some negotiation covering the whole status of Berlin, it is to me inconceivable that any settlement should not deal with the question of travel by DDR citizens abroad. TTDs are in any case an anachronism and at the very least I can only imagine that we should agree with the Russians on the terms on which they are issued. From this point of view, they are a wasting asset and it seems to me that we should be on sound ground if we said that we were imposing them until there was a satisfactory regulation of circulation questions in Berlin.

4. I really do not feel that we can do less than something like this or we shall be back in the old rut at a moment when we can certainly not afford such a situation.

12

Telegram from Sir C. Steel (Bonn) to the Foreign Office[1]

Tel. No. 787 *Priority Confidential*   BONN, 15 August 1961
                                                          D. 4.43 p.m.
                                                          R. 4.58 p.m.

Repeated for information to Washington, Paris and Saving to: Moscow
Berlin, UKDEL NATO, UKMIS New York, HQ BAOR and HQ RAF.

My telegram No. 785: Berlin.

Federal Government is urging calm on the West German population
and assuring them that the necessary counter-measures are being prepared.

2. On August 13 Dr Adenauer issued a statement calling for a firm but
calm response and Herr Strauss emphasized the need to avoid explosive
reactions, expressing his belief that there would not be war over Berlin. In
a nation wide television and radio programme on August 14 Dr Adenauer
again repeated emphatically that there was no cause for panic and said that
the Federal Government in the closest association with its allies would
master the situation. A Government spokesman announced on the same
day that appropriate counter-measures were being prepared and would
shortly be submitted to the North Atlantic Council. He did not go into
details, beyond saying that the measures would be 'adequate' and would
correspond in character to the Communist measures. The West would not
content itself with paper protests. At an election meeting on August 14 Dr
Adenauer referred to the possibility of a total NATO economic embargo
against the Soviet bloc if Khrushchev did not change his course in the
Berlin question. He emphasized that the West was united on the need to
take counter-measures and said that apart from these measures he
considered it necessary to examine the agreements existing between the
Federal Republic and the DDR. He also said that he did not give up hope
of 'sensible negotiations'.

3. There is no doubt that responsible German opinion of all shades
expects a rapid and effective reaction from the West. On August 14 the
dominant note in the Press comment was that this time protests, while
necessary, were not enough and that something had to be done. Today a
number of newspapers are already complaining of the delay in taking
action. Some take the line that the delay shows that the Western Powers
were not prepared for the latest East German measures. Others refer to

---

[1] DBPO Ser. 3 Vol. 6 No. 275; CG 10113/16.

signs that the West is prepared to accept the situation on the grounds that allied interests are allegedly not directly affected. In this connexion both Mr Rusk's statement of August 13 and the *Times* leading article of August 14 have been the subject of adverse comment. In a particularly strong leading article *Die Welt* says: 'if the Western Powers accept the aggravation of the situation which occurred on Sunday, they will have equally both weakened their own starting positions for future negotiations and have increased the aggressiveness of the other side'. *Neue Rhein Zeitung* says that if the West 'lets itself be lulled by a hypocritical respect for its rights of access, then soon it will be those rights which Moscow's salami tactics will attack'. *Mittag* asserts categorically that the West will accept the situation as it accepted the rape of Poland, Czechoslovakia and the Baltic States. Haffner's article referred to in my telegram under reference is also very bitter.

4. The editorials are generally not specific about the action they demand of the West, but most Bonn correspondents take it for granted that at least the issue of TTDs will be suspended.

5. Against this background the Federal Government will clearly find it more difficult to appeal for calm in the absence of any demonstrable evidence that the West is taking effective action.

13

Telegram from the Earl of Home to Sir H. Caccia (Washington)[1]

Tel. No. 5517 *Emergency Secret*   FOREIGN OFFICE, 15 August 1961
D: 6.35 p.m.

Repeated for information to: Paris, Bonn, Berlin, Moscow, UKDEL NATO and UKMIS New York.

Your telegrams Nos. 1925 and 1926 [of August 15: Berlin].

We think that it would be appropriate to protest both in Berlin and in Moscow. Clearly the Allied Commandants could not remain silent at such a moment without undermining morale in Berlin and we were glad to learn from the French Embassy here that the necessary instructions have now been sent to their representative.

2. At the same time I agree with the French that the Soviet Government must be left in no doubt about the serious view which our Governments take of recent developments and that our main protest should therefore be made in Moscow. As you know from our telegram No. 5493 we have been considering widening the scope of our demarche to include an offer of discussions of these and other questions relating to Germany but since this would inevitably delay things we are prepared, in the interests of speedy action, to accept the French draft subject to an amendment concerning the application of the 1949 agreements to freedom of movement within the city. (Foreign Office telegram to Berlin No. 145 makes the same point.) Please telegraph English text of further draft after your meeting.

3. We are anxious, however, that the Working Group should give consideration to the general idea of making use of the present situation as a peg on which to hang a proposal for talks. Bonn telegram No. 784 suggests that at least one of the objections to such an idea may not be as great as it seemed. It is also possible to argue that the knowledge that a proposal for discussion of the present situation had been made might help to reduce the chances of an upheaval in Eastern Germany. If you cannot appropriately float this idea at today's meeting, we suggest that you should do so tomorrow when you consider the United States draft reply to the latest Soviet note. Indeed it now seems to us that our reply to this note would be the better vehicle for conveying our ideas on East Germany to the Soviet Government. Please see my immediately following telegram.

---

[1] DBPO Ser. 3 Vol. 6 No. 278; CG 10113/27.

14

Telegram from the Earl of Home to Sir H. Caccia (Washington)[1]

Tel. No. 5518 *Emergency Secret*   FOREIGN OFFICE, 15 August 1961
                                                              D: 7.53 p.m.

Repeated for information to Paris, Bonn, Berlin, Moscow, UKDEL NATO and UKMIS New York

My immediately preceding telegram.

On the question of banning the issue of TTDs I still see the objections described in my telegram No. 1555 to Bonn. We must also keep our eye on the main objective which is to get an arrangement through negotiation which will guarantee the Western position in West Berlin, and the freedom and viability of West Berlin itself. We must not take any step which might make this more difficult, for example by inviting counter-measures from the Communist side, which by a process of escalation might take the issue out of our control.

2. However, I recognize that allied unity and promptness of action are of paramount importance in present circumstances and so long as all our Allies are satisfied that this step will not make the situation worse than it is, I am prepared to go along with them. We must insist, however, that the Federal Government should match the ban on TTDs by taking the necessary measures to prevent all East German travellers in prohibited categories from visiting the Federal Republic.

---

[1] DBPO Ser. 3 Vol. 6 No. 281; CG 10113/52.

15

Telegram from Sir H. Caccia (Washington) to the Foreign Office[1]

Tel. No. 1936 *Immediate Secret*   WASHINGTON, 15 August 1961
D: 16 August, 3.55 a.m.
R: 16 August, 4.20 a.m.

Repeated for information to Moscow, Paris, Bonn, Berlin, UKMIS New York and UKDEL NATO.

Your telegram No. 5517: Berlin: Protest in Moscow.

At an Ambassadorial group meeting this evening agreement was reached ad referendum on the text in my immediately following telegram. It is a composite effort based on the French draft. I have subsequently learnt that it has Mr Rusk's personal approval. It was agreed that three identical Notes should be delivered in Moscow on Thursday, August 17, and that the three Ambassadors should have discretion on the timing of delivery and the acceptance of minor amendments. I assume that you will send your instructions direct to Moscow.

2. It was agreed that the Press could be told of the fact of the delivery of a protest when it occurred, and that the texts should be released on Friday, August 18. The time proposed is 10 a.m., Washington time. I should be glad to know whether this is acceptable to you.

---

[1] DBPO Ser. 3 Vol. 6 No. 282; CG 10113/26.

16

Telegram from Sir H. Caccia (Washington) to the Foreign Office[1]

Tel. No. 1937 *Immediate Secret*   15 August 1961
                                                     D. 16 August, 4.25 a.m.
                                                     R. 16 August, 5.38 a.m.

Repeated for information to Moscow, Bonn, UKMIS New York, Paris, Berlin, UKDEL NATO

My immediately preceding telegram.

Following is text:

The British Embassy presents its compliments to the Minister for Foreign Affairs and upon instructions of its Government has the honour to direct the most serious attention of the Government of the U.S.S.R. to the following.

On August 13, East German authorities put into effect several measures regulating movement at the boundary of the Western sectors and the Soviet sector of the City of Berlin. These measures have the effect of limiting, to a degree approaching complete prohibition, passage from the Soviet sector to the Western sectors of the city. These measures were accompanied by the closing of the sector boundary by a sizeable deployment of police forces and by military detachments brought into Berlin for this purpose.

All this is a flagrant, and particularly serious, violation of the quadripartite status of Berlin. Freedom of movement with respect to Berlin was reaffirmed by the Quadripartite Agreement of New York of May 4, 1959, and by the decision taken at Paris on June 20, 1949, by the Council of the Ministers for Foreign Affairs of the Four Powers. Her Majesty's Government has never accepted that limitations can be imposed on freedom of movement within Berlin. The boundary between the Soviet sector and the Western sectors of Berlin is not a state frontier. Her Majesty's Government considers that the measures which the East German authorities have taken are illegal. It reiterates that it does not accept the pretension that the Soviet sector of Berlin forms a part of the so-called 'German Democratic Republic' and that Berlin is situated on its territory. Such a pretension is in itself a violation of the solemnly pledged word of the Government of the USSR in the agreement on the zones of occupation in Germany and the administration of Greater Berlin. Moreover, Her Majesty's Government cannot admit the right of the East

---

[1] DBPO Ser. 3, Vol. 6, No. 283; CG 10113/26.

German authorities to send their armed forces into the Soviet sector of Berlin.

By the very admission of the East German authorities, the measures which have just been taken are motivated by the fact that an ever increasing number of inhabitants of East Germany wish to leave this territory. The reasons for this exodus are known. They are simply the internal difficulties in East Germany.

To judge by the terms of a declaration of the Warsaw Pact Powers, published on August 13, the measures in question are supposed to have been recommended to the East German authorities by these Powers. Her Majesty's Government notes that the Powers which associated themselves with the USSR by signing the Warsaw Pact are thus intervening in a domain in which they have no competence.

It is to be noted that this declaration states that the measures taken by the East German authorities are 'in the interests of the German people themselves.' It is difficult to see any basis for this statement, or to understand why it should be for the members of the Warsaw Pact to decide what are the interests of the German people. It is evident that no Germans, particularly those whose freedom of movement is being forcibly restrained, think this is so. This would be abundantly clear if all Germans were allowed a free choice and the principle of self-determination were also applied in the Soviet sector of Berlin and in East Germany.

Her Majesty's Government solemnly protests against the measures referred to above, taken in an area for which the Soviet Government is responsible. Her Majesty's Government expects the Soviet Government to put an end to these illegal measures. This unilateral infringement of the quadripartite status of Berlin can only increase existing tension and dangers.

17

Telegram from Sir H. Caccia (Washington) to the Foreign Office[1]

Tel. No 1938 *Immediate Secret*   15 August 1961
D. 16 August, 4.50 a.m.
R. 16 August, 6.18 a.m.

Repeated for information to Paris, Bonn, Berlin, Moscow, UKDEL NATO, UKMIS New York.

Your telegram No. 5518: Berlin Counter Measures.

At the Ambassadorial Group Meeting this evening the German Ambassador, on instructions, pressed strongly for a ban on TTD's. He argued that a ban on TTD's was the nearest equivalent to the Soviet and East German action, and that it was a measure which really hurt the DDR He admitted there was a certain danger of escalation, but thought this was outweighed by the imperative need to take some action beyond mere protests. He foresaw the possibility of exceptions to the ban. He admitted that it might not cause the East Germans to revoke their measures, but it would be a useful counter in any negotiations.

2. In an equivocal statement, the French Chargé d'Affaires, on instructions, said that we must be careful to avoid giving the impression that we would tolerate a further move on the part of the Soviets or East Germans. On the other hand, we must not go so far as to incur a serious risk of escalation with the possibility of the cessation of civilian access to Berlin. At present economic counter-measures were too risky. In principle his Government could accept a complete ban on TTD's with exceptions to be worked out later. His immediate proposal, however, was that the Embassies in Bonn should be asked for an urgent report on the effectiveness and desirability of a ban on TTD's and on the possibility of closing the Allied Travel Office on the grounds of lack of customers (see paragraph 2 of my telegram No. 1925). Generally the French thought the whole attitude evinced by the Allies towards Moscow in the coming weeks was the main answer to the present East German action.

3. Her Majesty's Minister spoke in accordance with paragraph 1 of your telegram under reference and paragraph 3 of your telegram No. 1555 to Bonn, omitting the seventh, eighth and ninth sentences. He also broached the idea in paragraph 3 of your telegram No. 5517.

4. Mr Kohler in a strong statement said that after consideration in the

---

[1] DBPO Ser. 3, Vol. 6, No. 284; CG 10113/22.

Cabinet and at the 'highest level' the United States Government had concluded that none of the measures so far suggested was any good. None of them, including the ban on TTD's, would have any chance of causing an East German withdrawal and they would be laughed at by the Soviets. They might also lead to Soviet bloc reprisals. The United States Government was, however, very conscious of the need to reassure the population of West Berlin and to leave Moscow in no doubt of the seriousness with which the West regarded any infringement of the quadripartite agreements. Accordingly, the United States Government thought that if possible, all NATO Governments should take some positive action, but that this should not be announced as a reprisal for the East German action. He suggested the following:

(*a*) The United States forces in Berlin already made a practice of sending unarmed patrols through the Soviet Sector of Berlin to maintain in practice the concept of Berlin as a single city under quadripartite control. They proposed to increase these patrols, and urged that the British and French garrisons should do likewise.

(*b*) The Three Western Powers should make symbolic increases in their garrisons in West Berlin. There was no military reason for this, and the increases should be unprovocative, perhaps 1,000 United States Troops and 500 each French and British. This action, would, however, symbolize to the West Berliners the commitment of the West in their support.

(*c*) The most important step would be a drastic speed-up of the military build-up agreed upon in Paris. The United States had already announced its intentions in this regard, but was ready to make certain additional announcements about call-up training, etc. Perhaps other NATO countries could speed up the announcement of the steps they were proposing to take. The German Government in particular should consider the immediate introduction of a bill in the Bundestag extending conscription.

5. In addition, Mr Kohler said that he thought we should, in any case, instruct the Allied Travel Office to examine closely the reasons given by applicants for TTD's. We should not make it easy for these Germans to profit from the grant of TTD's. He suggested that without making any announcement all NATO Governments might refrain from granting visas to East Germans.

6. Mr Kohler said that the United States Government would like Allied and particularly German views on the probable psychological impact of the above measures. The French and German representatives and Her Majesty's Minister undertook to report. The German Ambassador stressed the importance of swift counter-measures, whatever they might be. I should be grateful for instructions.

Minute from Mr Watkinson (Minister of Defence) to Mr Macmillan[1]

Secret   16 August 1961

PRIME MINISTER

I had a meeting this afternoon with the Secretary of State for War, the Chiefs of Staff, and Sir Evelyn Shuckburgh, representing the Foreign Office, as I was most anxious to get the balance right in any announcements that we make over the next few days.

2. We must clearly now be seen to be doing enough without in any way being provocative or aggressive. On this basis, the War Office will announce tomorrow the initial moves from Hong Kong to the Middle East and from the Middle East to this country which form the start of the build-up of the reserve division. The Air Ministry will also announce the Javelin reinforcement for Germany and, if asked about the retention of the three fighter squadrons, will say these are being retained for the moment. These announcements should, I think, hold the position for this week. On Saturday, the War Office will announce the arrival in Berlin of the armoured vehicles which we have sent to General Delacombe to bring his vehicle complement up to strength. This I hope will satisfy the Americans that we are doing something to strengthen our Berlin garrison, as I am not anxious to send a further 500 men there if we can possibly avoid it. About the middle of next week, we shall need, I think, a further announcement if we are to hold the British and foreign press and stop accusations of 'dragging our feet'. I would, therefore, propose to announce the move of the Thunderbird regiment about the middle of the week because it will be necessary to give the executive order then in any case for the move to take place towards the end of September. Once this order is given, it is almost bound to leak and I would prefer to take the credit and have it properly announced by the War Office. This, I hope, will hold the position until the end of next week when we shall obviously have to think again in the light of the position as it then is. I will also send over to Admiralty House the more detailed instructions which cover these moves from the military and public relation points of view in case you would like to look at this as well.

---

[1] DBPO Ser. 3 Vol. 6 No. 289, CG 1016/97.

Telegram from the Earl of Home to Sir H. Caccia (Washington)[1]

Tel. No. 5541 *Immediate Secret*   FOREIGN OFFICE, 16 August 1961
D: 3.50 p.m.

Repeated for information to Moscow UKDEL NATO, Bonn and Berlin.

Washington telegram No. 1938 [August 15]: Berlin

In view of the mounting criticism at the failure of the Western Powers to react positively to the measures taken by the DDR, I think it is desirable that we should do at once those things which we can agree upon most easily.

2. I accept the text of the draft protest contained in Washington telegram No. 1937 and suggest that the protests should if possible be made in Moscow today rather than tomorrow. Please take this up immediately with the United States and French Governments and telegraph the result to Moscow, so that action may be put in train at once.

3. I would be willing to agree to the immediate imposition of a selective ban on TTDs on the lines suggested in Berlin telegram No. 285. This does not have the disadvantages of a total ban and would show public opinion in Germany and elsewhere that we are doing something. British representatives in the Allied Travel Office have authority to put these measures into effect as soon as French and American agreement has been obtained. In public we should take the line that we are not imposing a total ban because, unlike the East Germans, we do not wish to sever all contact between East and West Germany. It could be made known that we intend to apply much stricter standards than hitherto, especially in respect of persons associated with the East German régime, which is responsible for splitting Berlin.

4. The measures suggested by the Berlin Municipality (Berlin telegram No. 279) could if generally agreed be put into effect forthwith.

5. As regards the steps proposed by Mr Kohler (paragraph 4 of Washington telegram under reference) we hope to send you further instructions during the afternoon. As regards point (a) the desirability of increasing these patrols will presumably depend on the state of affairs on the sector borders. Local Commandants would have to exercise careful judgment to ensure that appearance of these patrols does not give rise to demonstrations in East Berlin. As regards British garrisons doing the

---

[1] DBPO Ser. 3 Vol. 6, No. 288; CG 10113/22.

same, this will presumably be dependent on issue of Sir C. Steel's discussions on the Brandenburg Gate on which see my telegram No. 155 to Berlin.

20

Telegram from Maj-Gen Delacombe (BMG Berlin) to the Foreign Office[1]

Tel. No. 291 *Immediate Secret*   BERLIN, 16 August 1961
D. 4.53 p.m.
R. 5.03 p.m.

Repeated for information to Washington, Bonn, UKDEL NATO, UKMIS New York, Paris, Moscow and HQ BAOR.

Washington telegram No. 1938: Berlin Counter Measures.
Following from Ambassador.
I arrived here this morning and have discussed the situation with GOC and McDermott. All, including Ledwidge, who has been here for five and-a-half years, are unanimous that the Berliners have been shaken to a greater extent than ever since 1948. Although I have not seen him yet, this seems to go for Brandt too. In the circumstances I cannot but feel that Kohler's analysis (Washington telegram under reference, paragraph 4) is very near the truth. I hope we shall embark soon on the modified TTD restrictions recommended in Berlin telegram No. 178, but I also think that a moderate military stiffening is probably far the best thing that could be done in present circumstances. Economic reprisals should clearly be reserved for defence of our access. It is a pity that the Chancellor has got them on the brain at the moment, but that need not worry us in the present situation. The demonstration of our continuing will to remain here and defend our rights ought to be much the best thing for local nerves.
2. General Delacombe tells me that as it happens a consignment of about forty mixed armoured vehicles is due to arrive on August 20. On being informed of this the American Commandant expressed admiration and envy and it seems to me that if we were to accompany these with a strong party of drivers, etc., but not more than about a hundred men, our demonstration of solidarity would be very reasonably covered. The Americans know how short we are and their chief interest is in the demonstration.
3. On a slightly longer term, I think that the knowledge that negotiations were to take place would have a more permanent calming effect, at least until the negotiations happen. What happens then will have

---

[1] DBPO Ser. 3 Vol. 6 No. 291, CG 10113/30.

to be faced in any case, and it may be that the present shock to German complacency may have done some good after all.

Telegram from Sir F. Roberts (Moscow) to the Foreign Office[1]

Tel. No. 1514 *Immediate Secret*   MOSCOW, 16 August 1961
D. 5.06 p.m.
R. 5.36 p.m.

Repeated for information to Washington, Paris, Berlin, Bonn and UKDEL NATO.

Washington telegram No. 1938: Berlin.

I agree that the Soviet Government are unlikely to be much impressed by relative pin-pricks like a ban on TTDs, but nor do I think that Khrushchev would be at all impressed by Mr Kohler's proposals (*a*) and (*b*). He is a realist, who accepts the symbolic importance of maintaining Western garrisons in Berlin but also knows his own strength locally. To add two thousand would not, in his view, strengthen our position; it would only add so many more useless hostages in the event of serious trouble. Nor would he be likely to pay any attention to increased patrolling, unless it was increased to the point of becoming a serious irritant to which he would be compelled to react. Such moves from weakness may be useful for Berlin morale, but they suggest to me a complete misunderstanding of present Soviet psychology and of the real position in and around Berlin.

2. There is rather more sense in (*c*) as a deterrent, although here again there is surely a contradiction between what I understood to be the Western policy of a quiet and orderly build-up, which would be observed by the Russians, without forcing them to react with public statements or a similar build-up and this new insistence upon accelerated public statements and public emphasis upon Western military measures. We should not overlook the fact that the Russians have been careful to stop the refugee flow by measures on their side of the Iron Curtain and have done nothing yet to interfere with West Berlin and its communications, nor with Western rights and communications.

---

[1] DBPO Ser. 3 Vol. 6 No. 292, CG 10113/22.

Telegram from Sir C. Steel (Bonn) to the Foreign Office[1]

Tel. No.796 *Priority Confidential*   BONN, 16 August 1961
                                                                     D.7.18 p.m.
                                                                     R.7.30 p.m.

Repeated for information to Washington, Berlin, Paris, and Saving to Moscow, UKMIS New York, HQ RAF Germany, UKDEL NATO and HQ BAOR.

My telegram No.787: Berlin.
The general atmosphere here is still very worked up.
2. The Bundestag has been recalled for a special session on August 18 at which the Federal Government will make a statement on Berlin. It is reported that this will contain an explanation of the counter-measures which the Federal Government is to take. A Government spokesman said on August 15 that in addition to the joint measures already under discussion the Federal Government were preparing counter-measures which are within their own competence. He gave no details but emphasised that all proposals for counter-measures would be discussed with the Western Allies. The Federal Government was guided by its responsibilities towards all Germans and would take no step which could have unforeseeable consequences.
3. The German Press has published under bold headlines very detailed stories from Washington and London describing American and British reluctance to take drastic counter-measures at this stage. The general feeling is summed up in the *Bild* headline 'The West does *nothing.* President Kennedy is silent. Macmillan goes shooting. Adenauer calls Brandt names'. (A reference to an election speech on which I am reporting separately).
4. German opinion is in fact still in favour of reacting sharply. Dr Krone the Chairman of the CDU Parliamentary party who has just returned from two days in Berlin, tells us that the West Berliners are incensed over the Communist measures but are also incensed and disappointed over what they believe to be the unpreparedness of the Western Powers and their failure to respond adequately. He added that these feelings of anger and disappointment were shared by his own party and, he thought, in the Federal Republic as a whole.

---

[1] DBPO Ser. 3 Vol. 6 No. 295, CG 10113/16.

5. Feeling seems to be running high in the Bundestag where Committee meetings are taking place today, and the general opinion is that the West has shown itself inadequate in the present situation. We are of course urging restraint. Fortunately proceedings on August 18 will consist only of a government declaration followed by short statements by each party, without debate. Statements will no doubt be carefully worded but it may be difficult for them to conceal the bitterness with which the Parliament views the present situation.

23

Telegram from the Foreign Office to Sir H. Caccia (Washington)[1]

Tel. No. 5553 *Immediate Secret*   FOREIGN OFFICE, 16 August 1961
D. 7.18 p.m.

Repeated for information to Bonn, Berlin, Paris, UKDEL NATO, Immediate to Moscow and UKMIS New York.

Your telegram No. 1938 [of August 16] Berlin counter-measures.

We have now given consideration to the proposals outlined in paragraph 4 and following is additional information which you can use in discussion in the four-power group tonight:

(*a*) Comments already telegraphed to Bonn about the idea of additional unarmed patrols in East Berlin are confirmed. This must be carefully handled on the spot. Sir C. Steel may wish to consider whether he himself (and/or any other Western personalities now in Berlin) should seek opportunity to drive over the sector border.

(*b*) We intend to send up to West Berlin on the night of August 18th, 18 one-ton armoured vehicles and 16 ferret armoured cars. Routine announcement to this effect will be made by War Office on the following day. We consider this reinforcement, which has been under consideration recently, constitutes the best 'symbolic increase' in our garrison in West Berlin that we can make at the present time. We think it should be more effective than sending additional men which could only go at the expense of BAOR.

(*c*) As regards our military build up, as announced by the Secretary of State to the Foreign Ministers in Paris, following speed-up programme of announcements is now contemplated:

(i) Air Ministry will announce to-morrow the impending reinforcement of Javelin force in Germany. For your own information this comprises reinforcements of existing squadrons by individual aircraft. In answer to Press enquiries the Ministry of Defence will confirm that this is one step in a programme of wider measures designed to increase British capabilities in Germany and will also reveal that the three squadrons which were to have been withdrawn at the end of the year will now be retained in Germany.

(ii) War Office will announce, also this week, the return of the 3rd Dragoon Guards to the United Kingdom to form part of the division being

---

[1] DBPO Ser. 3, Vol. 6, No. 294; CG 1016/85.

constituted from the Strategic Reserve: in answer to questions, certain consequential moves of armour from Hong Kong to the Middle East will be revealed.

(iii) Announcement will probably be made (this is still subject to final ministerial approval) that move of SAGW regiment to Germany has been ordered for the end of September.

Telegram from Maj-Gen Delacombe (BMG Berlin) to the Foreign Office[1]

No. 292 *Immediate Confidential*   BERLIN, 17 August 1961
D: 11.45 a.m.
R: 11.48 a.m.

Repeated for information to Foreign Office, HQ BAOR, HQ RAF Germany, Washington, Paris, UKDEL NATO and Moscow.

Your telegram No. 53: Brandenburg Gate.

As agreed with the Ambassador, British troops began putting up a barbed wire fence around the Soviet War Memorial in the British sector at 0400 hours August 17. There will be a gap in the fence to allow passage to the Soviet guard. British guards will be posted at each corner.

2. At the same hour I sent the following telephone message to the Soviet Commandant.

Begins:

In view of the present situation I am taking measures to give extra protection to the Soviet Memorial in the British sector.

Ends.

3. Symbolic effect of fencing in the memorial should cheer up the Berliners. It also has a real value as a protective measure. The memorial has occasionally been the target of anti-Soviet gestures at times of tension in the past. The Soviet Commandant asked General Rome to take protective measures during demonstrations over the Hungarian rising in 1956.

4. We shall explain the action to the Press as a protective measure which will last as long as necessary.

---

[1] DBPO Ser. 3 Vol. 6 No. 297; CG 10113/24.

Telegram from Sir H. Caccia (Washington) to the Foreign Office[1]

Tel. No. 1960 *Emergency Secret*
WASHINGTON, 17 August 1961
D: 18 August 1961, 1.52 a.m.
R: 18 August 1961, 2.15 a.m.

Repeated for information to Bonn, Berlin, Paris, UKDEL NATO, Moscow and Berlin.

Mr Rusk summoned me and my French and German colleagues this evening to tell us that at his meeting with the President this afternoon the following action had been decided in order to reassure the West Berliners:

(*a*) the President was sending a message to the Prime Minister and General de Gaulle suggesting that they should jointly issue a statement, the draft of which is attached to the message, reaffirming their Berlin commitments. The message to the Prime Minister is being transmitted through the United States Embassy in London. Mr Rusk hoped the Prime Minister's reply would be available tomorrow so that the text of the tripartite statement could be finally agreed and issued as soon as possible, either tomorrow, Friday afternoon, or Saturday,

(*b*) the United States Government have decided to reinforce their Berlin garrison by a battle group (1,500 to 1,800 men) drawn from their existing forces in Germany. It will move up the Autobahn. Mr Rusk hoped that Her Majesty's Government and the French Government would take comparable action. I reminded Mr Rusk of the reinforcements which we had already decided to send to Berlin tomorrow night but he hoped that we would consider sending a further unit—perhaps a reinforced battalion.

(*c*) the Vice-President, probably accompanied by General Clay, will go to Berlin this weekend to deliver personally the President's reply to Herr Brandt's message. The Vice-President will also pay a call on Chancellor Adenauer.

---

[1] DBPO Ser. 3 Vol. 6 No. 302, CG 10113/40.

Minute by Mr J. N. Henderson (Northern Department)[1]

Secret   FOREIGN OFFICE, 18 August 1961

Current Indications of Soviet tactics over Germany and Berlin

The frontier restrictions imposed in Berlin on August 12 were obviously decided upon in principle by the Warsaw Pact Meeting in Moscow, August 3-5, which appears to have been held in secrecy and haste. They seem to have been dictated solely by the deteriorating refugee situation.

2. The extent to which the Russians are probably embarrassed by this step, wish to keep it in a low key, and regard it as outside their original plan of campaign for Berlin, is indicated by:

(*a*) the markedly defensive treatment of the subject in the Soviet Press and Radio;

(*b*) the silence of Soviet leaders on the subject (Khrushchev is on holiday at the Black Sea, where he intends to remain until early September, i.e. until Nehru comes to Moscow from the Belgrade Conference);

(*c*) the absence of any important Soviet military measures, apart from some small-scale deployment intended as backing for the refugee controls;

(*d*) the assurance reported to have been given by the Soviet Ambassador to Dr Adenauer that Khrushchev did not intend doing anything to aggravate the Berlin situation before the West Berlin elections;

(*e*) the relative mildness and defensive character of the Soviet Commandant's reply of August 15 to the Western Commandants' letters of protest about the new restrictions.

3. There is no reason to suppose that the imposition of the Berlin frontier controls betokens a deliberate acceleration in the Soviet time-table for the solution of the Berlin problem. For:

(i) If the Soviet Government were to go ahead now and sign a peace treaty, this would be a contradiction of everything that Khrushchev and other leaders have been saying for a long time.

(ii) Khrushchev probably still wants to go through the motions of enabling the maximum number of other powers to attend the peace conference, and he knows perfectly well that nothing is possible on the Western side until at any rate after the German elections.

(iii) The East German Foreign Minister, Bolz, declared in the Volkskammer on August 11 that by the decision of the recent Warsaw Pact

---

[1] DBPO Ser. 3 Vol. 6 No. 305, CG 10113/77.

Meeting the Foreign Ministers of the Socialist states would meet in the late autumn to discuss the preparatory work for the conclusion of a peace treaty (i.e. there was no question of a peace treaty in the immediate future).

4. The question arises whether the imposition of the Berlin frontier controls, even though it may not indicate a shift in the Soviet time-table, can be expected to have an effect on Khrushchev's readiness to negotiate. It has been suggested that the growth in tension which is likely to occur in East Germany as a result of the closure of the escape route may induce the Russians to negotiate sooner rather than later, so as to avoid the difficulties and odium which would result from having to supress an uprising. But it is submitted that the population of East Germany know perfectly well that any uprising is likely to be of no use, and the Russians are probably not particularly nervous that one will occur. What Khrushchev will have in the front of his mind, surely, is the need to enter negotiation on the best possible footing. To start talks in the immediate aftermath of the controls and with the refugee question uppermost would be obviously disadvantageous from his point of view. It is much more in his interest to leave the present situation as it is at any rate for a few weeks, in the hope that it will have been tacitly accepted by all parties before negotiations begin.

5. On the other hand—if this is not irrelevant—it does seem that from the West's stand-point the fact that the refugee question has been solved by fait accompli makes our negotiating position somewhat easier. The DDR will no longer be able to point to the need to stop the refugee loophole as the reason for controlling Western access to Berlin. Equally, we will not in our requirements have to ensure that in making even minimum de facto recognition of the DDR control we are not thereby prejudicing the highly sensitive question of refugees.

27

Telegram from Sir C. Steel (Bonn) to the Foreign Office[1]

Tel. No. 805 *Priority Secret*   BONN, 18 August 1961
                                                                      D: 2.05 p.m.
                                                                      R: 2.22 p.m.

Repeated for information to Washington, Paris, Moscow, UKDEL NATO, Berlin, HQ BAOR and HQ RAF (Germany).

Berlin
As I understand you will be in London over the weekend, you may like to have a short account of my impressions of Berlin.

2. The first impact of the sealing of the sector border has been very severe and has produced a considerable fall in Berlin morale. Given the ignorance of the real Power relationships which has been fostered by the political leadership under Dulles's inspiration over many years this is not surprising. Nor is it surprising that fear and exasperation should express themselves in resentment of the Western Allies. Nevertheless, when I drove around in both halves of the city for more than two hours yesterday life looked surprisingly normal everywhere except at the barriers and I have a feeling that the first upsurge of popular passion is subsiding. The weekend will show whether this is really so.

3. On the other hand, this is not a situation which should be allowed to drift. We shall need the combative and durable qualities of the Berlin population very much over the coming months and I think it is essential to re-establish the relationship of confidence which has existed up till now. The measures contemplated by the Americans for this purpose seem to me on the right lines. I put it to Brandt yesterday that reassertion of our determination to stay in Berlin and concrete measures in this direction would be much better than any kind of reprisal. He agreed and, in particular, ruled out economic action for the same reasons that we do. What worries him are the longer term economic prospects. He fears that the events of the last few days will encourage the migration of both capital and labour to the West, increase the unviability of the city and lay it further open to the attempts which he is sure will be made to make its economy dependent on the East. We shall have to think about this.

4. On the wider front, I am confirmed in my feeling that the prospect of negotiations would have a calming effect on the situation in Berlin, but

---

[1] DBPO Ser. 3 Vol. 6 No. 306, CG 10113/48.

it may be more difficult to secure acquiescence in the sort of concessions which we will have to make for agreement. The recent shock may, however, bring a greater sense of realism and be helpful. I think people are expecting negotiations and Smirnov's visit to Adenauer is certainly significant. Even from what we have been told of the interview, and I should not think we have been told everything, it is obvious that the Russian aim was to reassure Adenauer and to prevent their action in Berlin from spoiling the prospects for a negotiation. Their estimate of the situation in the DDR must, indeed, have been bad for them to allow this to happen in the middle of their general Berlin campaign. I should think that if some programme for negotiation were now set, even if no actual meeting took place for several weeks, things should be calm until then. Much would depend, of course, on whether the Russians continued their tactics of intimidation in too high a key, but we might perhaps frighten them off this by threatening not to meet them at all.

5. In conclusion, I should like to say a word about the General and his staff in Berlin. They and Brandt's good sense have probably been the greatest stabilizing factors in the situation and Delacombe's good temper and imperturbability have been an example.

28

Telegram from the Foreign Office to Sir H. Caccia (Washington)[1]

Tel. No. 5634 *Immediate Secret*   FOREIGN OFFICE, 18 August 1961
D: 9.05 p.m.

Repeated for information to Paris, Bonn, Berlin, UKDEL NATO and Moscow.

My telegram No. 5608 [of August 18].
Please deliver as soon as possible to the President the following reply from the Prime Minister.

Dear Mr President,
Thank you for your letter and for the draft of the declaration which you suggest that President de Gaulle and you and I might make. No doubt you will consider very carefully before you finally decide whether it is likely to be counter-productive. So far, Mr Khrushchev has put himself very much in the wrong with world opinion and we do not want the blame to be switched from the Russians and East Germans on the ground that we are being entirely negative in our approach to the problem.
If you feel after consideration that there should be a declaration I would be willing to join in one worded as follows:
Begins:
'The action of the East German authorities and of the Soviet Government in closing off the Eastern sector of Berlin, and other measures of restraint instituted by them to limit the freedom of movement of the people under their control, have seriously and dangerously increased tension in Berlin.
The President of the United States, the President of France and the Prime Minister of the United Kingdom feel it necessary in the light of these actions to issue a solemn warning concerning the determination of their countries to maintain their rights, to fulfil their obligations to those under their protection and to preserve the freedom and viability of West Berlin and the right of access to and from the West.'
Ends.
I hope you will feel this contains the essential points which will help to reassure the West Berliners.

---

[1] DBPO Ser. 3 Vol. 6 No. 309; CG 10113/43.

I am sure that, if we do make a declaration, we should let it be known simultaneously that we are ready to begin exploring the modalities of negotiations. Our Ambassador has been instructed to make this point in the Ambassadorial Group meeting which takes place this afternoon.

I have also considered your suggestion for further reinforcements of the Garrison in Berlin. As you know, we have already arranged to send in some armoured vehicles. These are on their way by train and their arrival should be a tangible sign to the West Berliners of our continued concern for their liberty. We are not inclined at the moment to send a detached battalion from the United Kingdom and if we sent any reinforcements to Berlin from Western Germany this would weaken our formations without, I feel, any corresponding military advantage.

With warm regards,
Yours sincerely,
Harold Macmillan.

2. Please see my immediately following telegram.

Telegram from the Earl of Home to Sir H. Caccia (Washington)[1]

Tel. No. 5635 *Immediate Secret*   FOREIGN OFFICE, 18 August 1961
D: 9.15 p.m.

Repeated for information Immediate to Paris, Bonn, Berlin, UKDEL NATO and Moscow.

My immediately preceding telegram.

The text of the proposed declaration in the Prime Minister's message combines paragraphs 2 and 3 of the President's draft. These seemed somewhat repetitive and the wording now follows more closely the three principles which Mr Rusk, M. Couve de Murville and I agreed during our meetings in Paris. I want it to be clear too that we are fulfilling existing obligations to the people of West Berlin, rather than undertaking new ones. We also think it better to omit the words 'at whatever cost' which might cause unnecessary alarm at this stage.

2. I have not yet learnt President de Gaulle's definite reactions to President Kennedy's proposal. I attach importance, however, to there being an agreed declaration issued in the names of the three heads of government rather than three separate and possibly different declarations issued individually in the three capitals. The latter alternative could give great scope for wedge-driving between the Allies, and would not ensure that we get any amendments at all to the present American draft. If President de Gaulle refuses to co-ordinate his text, I still think it most important that at least we and the Americans should issue identical declarations.

3. I also attach great importance to an announcement being made at about the same time as the issue of this declaration to the effect that we are seriously considering the modalities of negotiations and that instructions have been sent to the Western Ambassadors in Moscow to get in touch with the Soviet Government about this (paragraph 4 of my telegram No. 5602 to you). I think therefore that the whole question of the timing of these moves, including arrangements for simultaneous release of the declarations, should be discussed and co-ordinated in Washington.

4. I leave it to you to decide whether you make these points to the President himself or to Mr Rusk.

---

[1] DBPO Ser. 3 Vol. 6 No. 310; CG 10113/43.

Telegram from Sir A. Rumbold (Paris) to the Foreign Office[1]

Tel. No. 477 *Emergency Secret*   PARIS, 18 August 1961
                                                            D. 9.20 p.m.
                                                            R. 9.27 p.m.

Repeated for information to Washington, Bonn, Berlin, Moscow and Saving to UKDEL NATO.

Sir A. Rumbold's telegram No. 476: Berlin.

The Secretary-General has now given me President de Gaulle's reply to Mr Kennedy's message which is at the moment being telegraphed to Washington. M. Chauvel is being instructed to give you the text first thing tomorrow.

Following is quick translation:

'Having received your message of today, I gladly agree to join with you and, contingently, with Mr Macmillan in a common declaration on Berlin. I am sending you herewith the text I propose and which, except for the ending which I think it well to add, differs little from the one you sent me.

It will certainly not escape you that this enterprise, once undertaken by the three of us in such a solemn manner, could not be, henceforth, be got out of (*remis en cause*). In particular, I do not well see what would be the object of a negotiation on Berlin with Moscow embarked upon now, once our position is going to be so categorically decided upon and published. As you know, France, without being opposed, (indeed the contrary), to the principle of a negotiation, believes that one cannot be engaged upon usefully unless the international atmosphere has first of all been changed profoundly; that is to say made peaceful instead of being threatening. I believe we should say so'.

My immediately following telegram contains proposed text.

---

[1] DBPO Ser. 3 Vol. 6 No. 311; CG 10113/43.

31

Telegram from Sir F. Roberts (Moscow) to the Foreign Office[1]

Tel. No. 1531 *Immediate Confidential*   MOSCOW, 18 August 1961
                                                                           D: 11.39 p.m.
                                                                           R: 11.58 p.m.

Repeated for information Priority to Paris Bonn, Berlin, UKDEL NATO, Washington and Berlin.

Berlin.
Seven page Note was delivered at 7 p.m. GMT by Soviet Ministry of Foreign Affairs containing reply to our Note of August 17.

2. It supports actions of DDR in establishing effective control of frontier with West Berlin, makes familiar accusations against misuse of West Berlin for espionage, propaganda, militarism and other activities directed against DDR and accuses Federal Government of exercising unwarranted control of West Berlin.

3. Note claims that three Western Governments have admitted that West Berlin is not part of Federal Republic, but, despite Soviet complaints, Western occupation authorities have tolerated illegal activities of Federal agencies in Berlin. DDR have shown great tolerance, but this has not prevented attempts to undermine its achievements and interests, more especially since announcement of the necessity for an early peace treaty.

4. Her Majesty's Government having violated the four-Power agreement, insist upon those parts which suit their interests. Berlin currency arrangements, the bi-zone, the three-Power arrangements in Berlin and the Paris agreements of 1954 are quoted as flagrant violations of four-Power agreements. These were based upon post-war occupation needs. Much has changed in sixteen years and two separate German States now exist, into whose internal affairs outside interference is no longer permissible.

5. If recent 'defence measures' on sector boundary creates temporary inconveniences for Berlin population, blame rests upon Western Governments and Federal Government, who have prevented regularisation of situation. Our protest is therefore categorically rejected.

6. Last paragraph repeats that DDR's measures are temporary and that Soviet Government has repeatedly stressed that Peace Treaty and normalisation on that basis of West Berlin situation will not infringe

---

[1] DBPO Ser. 3 Vol. 6 No. 303, CG 10113/52.

interests of either side and will promote general peace and security, to which Her Majesty's Government are also committed.

7. Translation follows in my immediately following telegram.

8. French Ambassador has told me that Sobolev this evening dismissed our Notes as a propaganda exercise and complained that they contained no positive proposals for improving the situation.

32

Telegram from Sir H. Caccia (Washington) to the Foreign Office[1]

Tel. No. 1976 *Immediate Secret*   WASHINGTON, 18 August 1961
                                                                         D. 19 August, 2.12 a.m.
                                                                         R. 19 August, 3 a.m.

Repeated for information to Paris, UKDEL NATO, Berlin, Bonn and Moscow.

Your telegrams Nos. 6534 and 5635: Berlin.

I took the Prime Minister's message down to the White House, where the President was in conference with the Vice-President and others prior to the latter's departure tonight for Berlin. Mr Rusk and Mr Kohler came out of the meeting to see me and I handed the Prime Minister's message to them and made the points in your second telegram under reference. Mr Rusk was then called back to the President and the subsequent conversation took place with Mr Kohler alone.

2. He expressed some disappointment that we were not prepared to send reinforcements to Berlin beyond the armoured vehicles which are going in tonight. His main concern, however, centred on the link we wished to establish between the issue of a tripartite statement and of an announcement that instructions were being sent to the Western Ambassadors in Moscow to get into touch with the Soviet Government about the modalities of negotiations. Apart from the difficulty of getting the French to agree to this, Mr Kohler was disinclined to connect the timing of the two moves, which were directed to different audiences and were in a different order of urgency. The first was designed to meet the immediate needs of the situation in Berlin. It might indeed prepare the way for the second move the desirability of which he did not contest but which he thought could only emerge as a result of further discussions. These ought certainly to be pursued urgently, but they could not possibly be completed this weekend.

3. As we were talking, Mr Kohler received a telephone message from the State Department to say that General de Gaulle's reply had just been received. He promised to get into touch with me when the President had had time to consider the Prime Minister's message and General de Gaulle's reply.

---

[1] DBPO Ser. 3 Vol. 6 No. 312, CG 10113/43.

33

Telegram from Sir. F. Roberts (Moscow) to the Foreign Office[1]

Tel. No. 1534 *Immediate Secret*   MOSCOW, 19 August 1961
                                                                    D. 11.24 a.m.
                                                                    R. 11.30 a.m.

Repeated for information to Washington, Paris, Bonn, Berlin and UKDEL NATO.

Berlin.

I submit that it is important at this juncture to guard against the danger that the exercise of reassuring the Berliners and maintaining West German morale might take us so far that it forced a response from Khrushchev which would still further increase tension and involve us all in political and possibly military escalation.

2. Since the closing of the sector frontier the Russians have, for obvious reasons, been playing the crisis down, while asserting that the Western Powers are being dragged into hysterical and dangerous courses by the West Germans, although Western rights etc. in and around Berlin have not been touched. Smirnov's attitude with Adenauer seems to have been moderate and even reassuring. The general impression created here, and accepted by several of my more reasonably allied and 'neutral' colleagues, is that the Russians are now looking to negotiations after the German elections, in which they will be prepared to take a reasonable line. The Russians lose no opportunity to tell us that they are awaiting Western proposals.

3. Is there not a real danger that the top-level tripartite declaration now proposed by Washington may either

(*a*) provoke further action or at least some violent counter-declaration by Khrushchev, or

(*b*) enable him to pose before the world as the injured party?

Khrushchev might feel compelled or think the opportunity too good to miss to carry out his suspended plans

(*a*) to move divisions to the Western frontiers of the Soviet Union, and

(*b*) to put war factories on an eight-hour day.

4. From the Moscow angle I should hope that the steps already canvassed, and more especially the Vice-President's visit to Berlin and Bonn and the move of fifteen hundred United States reinforcements down

---

[1] DBPO Ser. 3 Vol. 6 No. 313, CG 10113/45.

the Autobahn, would be enough to sustain Berlin and West German morale and that the additional statement by three Heads of Government could be kept in reserve for some later stage in what promises to be a prolonged crisis. Incidentally, a public statement of this kind would not, in my judgment, create the best psychological atmosphere in which to carry out the proposed Ambassadorial probe with Khrushchev.

34

Telegram from Maj-General Delacombe (BMG Berlin) to the
Foreign Office[1]

Tel. No. 304 *Priority Confidential*   BERLIN, 19 August 1961
D: 6.00 p.m.
R: 8.05 p.m.

Addressed to Bonn No. 197, repeated for information to Foreign Office, Washington, Paris and UKDEL NATO.

Your telegram No. 56.

Restrictions on West Berliners visiting East Berlin have progressively increased, first by reduction of crossing points to thirteen, then to twelve, (when the Tor was 'temporarily' closed). Now West Berliners travelling by car must obtain a permit which can be obtained at only three points. According to West Berlin police yesterday, at one of these points West Berlin drivers are turned back; at another they are told to apply for a pass, the issue of which takes five-six days; while at the third only West Berlin drivers employed in East Berlin are permitted to pass. However, the situation at the crossing points is still fluid and preliminary police report today suggests that West Berliners working in East Berlin may cross at more than one crossing point. Interpretation of 'revanchists' seems to be becoming stricter. Cardinal Doepfner was prevented from crossing by car, but allowed on foot; Kressmann, Mayor of Kreuzberg, was prevented on August 17 from crossing at all. Bishop Dibelius, who was allowed to cross by car on August 14, was prevented on August 17 from crossing at all. All West Berliners are required to fill in a form; some have been searched and some turned back. As to the S and U-Bahns, two S-Bahn lines which now begin in West Berlin converge while still in West Berlin and terminate at Friedrichstrasse (East Berlin), while one U-Bahn line running from north to south in West Berlin passes through East Berlin, where trains stop only at Friedrichstrasse. Controls at Friedrichstrasse are strict.

2. The East Germans already are anxious to reduce and control strictly the entry of West Berliners into East Berlin. In estimating how far they can go they are no doubt strongly influenced by the reaction or lack of reaction to each previous step. It seems doubtful whether such restrictions will be automatically relaxed if the crisis dies away (which is itself unlikely, anyway for some time). Rather we would expect the East

---

[1] DBPO Ser. 3 Vol. 6 No. 319; CG 10113/46.

Germans to retain the highest degree of restriction they can get away with, so as to keep up their sleeve relaxations which are not vital to them and which could be made at some later stage for tactical reasons, for example to demonstrate that signing of a peace treaty had led to certain relaxations. We are inclined to doubt whether they aim to stop all access by West Berliners to East Berlin. In so far as it permits some innocuous visiting between relatives, it is still a sort of safety valve.

3. As regards West Germans visiting East Berlin, the number of points at which they are permitted to cross has been reduced to four ('temporarily' three), but we have not yet heard of any West Germans being refused entry. West Germans, unlike West Berliners, do not need to get a permit to bring in their cars, but merely have to accept a personal *'passierschein'*.

4. Leopold's original 'expectations' with regard to the *passierschein* decree were, in any event, drastically modified when the practical (not legal) facilitation of the *passierschein* procedure introduced on February 15 was tacitly accepted as satisfactory. To the extent that reduction of number of crossing points indicates that controls on visiting West Germans are no longer perfunctory, even this modified 'expectation' has been disappointed, if not contravened. However, West Berlin police report that West German vehicles are cleared generally quickly and promptly. It appears, however, that in some cases the drivers are obliged to leave their vehicles to obtain *passierscheine*. But it is difficult to establish factually the precise extent of increased inconvenience to West German visitors.

5. Movement between the Federal Republic and West Berlin has not been interfered with, though lorries have been searched for refugees, after which they have been permitted to pass through East German controls without further difficulty. Where the lorries searched were officially sealed on entering the DDR (and this never became a universal practice), this constitutes a technical violation of the 'expectations'. The East Germans would, no doubt, argue that this action has become necessary under new conditions which were not obtaining at the time of the Leopold agreement.

6. For what it is worth, Leopold's own view is that the expectations have not (repeat not) been contravened. He regards treatment of West German visitors as substantially unchanged so far by the new restrictions, and points out that movement of West Berliners into East Berlin was, in any event, not covered by the agreement.

35

Telegram from Sir H. Caccia (Washington) to the Foreign Office[1]

Tel. No. 1981 *Immediate Secret*   WASHINGTON, 19 August 1961
                                                                                    D. 6.53 p.m.
                                                                                    R. 7.10 p.m.

Repeated for information to Paris, Berlin, Moscow, Bonn and UKDEL NATO.

My telegram No. 1976: Berlin.

As the comments of the Prime Minister and General de Gaulle were so divergent, the President has dropped the idea of a tripartite statement.

2. I obtained this information from the State Department before receipt of your telegram No. 5652. In the circumstances I do not propose to take any action on your telegram today, but will be guided by it at the meeting of the Ambassadorial Group on Monday.

---

[1] DBPO Ser. 3 Vol. 6 No. 320; CG 10113/43.

36

**Telegram from Mr Tomlinson (UKDEL NATO, Paris)
to the Foreign Office**[1]

Tel. No. 109 *Immediate Secret*   PARIS, 19 August 1961
                                                        D. 8.23 p.m.
                                                        R. 8.35 p.m.

Repeated for information to Bonn, Moscow, Washington and Saving to Paris, UKMIS New York and Berlin.

Berlin.

At a meeting of the Council held this afternoon at the request of the United States Delegation, Durbrow explained the reasons for the United States decision to strengthen their garrison in Berlin by one battle group and gave the Council details of the composition of the battle group and the timing of the move. He emphasised that the move was nothing more than an 'administrative strengthening' of the United States garrison designed to stiffen the morale of the West Berliners. He also referred to the President's decision to send Vice-President and General Clay to Berlin. He explained that it had been the United States intention to inform the Council of these decisions before they were announced but an unfortunate leakage had made this impossible.

2. The Secretary-General stressed that the United States move was in no sense a probe and was not intended to be provocative. If, however, any attempt were made to hinder the passage of the United States battle group we should clearly enter a new phase. So far, the vital interests of the West as defined by Mr Rusk when he spoke to the Council on August 8, had not been infringed. They certainly would be if the battle group were stopped. It was right, therefore, that the Council had been given this important information and some members might think that the Council should have been consulted before the decision was taken. Mr Stikker went on to refer to the Council's programme of work in relation to Berlin and said that if duplication were to be avoided there must be co-ordination between the Council and the working group. The Council was in urgent need of more information about the progress made in the Working Group.

3. The ensuing discussion showed some misunderstanding on the part of several members of the purposes of the United States move and some disposition to bear that there might be serious incidents when the battle

---

[1] DBPO Ser. 3 Vol. 6 No. 321; CG 1016/86.

group reached Helmstedt. While not excluding the possibility of incidents, I therefore reminded the Council that there was no international agreement limiting the size of the Western garrisons in Berlin and that military traffic, including rotations of sizeable units, was flowing normally. I then made a distinction between:

(*a*) the general NATO military build-up which was designed to have an impact on the Soviet Authorities and to improve the bargaining position of the West in the event of negotiations and,

(*b*) immediate military moves such as those under discussion which were designed to reassure the population of West Berlin.

4. Under (*b*) Her Majesty's Government had considered what steps they could take at once which would not weaken BAOR and be of a kind to make an impact on the population of Berlin. I then informed the Council of our decision to send armoured vehicles to Berlin and said that since they were due to leave last night, I assumed, although I was without confirmation, that they had already arrived.

5. The French representative said that although his Government had reached no final decision they were contemplating sending three companies of parachute troops—about one thousand men—to Berlin. He hoped that he would be able to give the Council more definite information about this on August 21.

Please see my immediately following telegram.

Telegram from Sir C. Steel (Bonn) to the Foreign Office[1]

Tel. No. 818 *Priority Secret*   BONN, 21 August 1961
D: 6.05 p.m.
R: 7.07 p.m.

Repeated for information to Washington, UKDEL NATO, Moscow, Paris and Berlin.

Washington telegram No. 1981.

I think it is an excellent thing that the declaration has been dropped. There seems no doubt that the Johnson visit to Berlin has triggered a very satisfactory reaction in Berlin and West German opinion, and we should be content to leave it at that. There is no point at present in further bolstering Berlin morale, which is far too addicted to a diet of gestures.

---

[1] DBPO Ser. 3 Vol. 6 No. 323; CG 10113/43.

38

Telegram from Sir F. Roberts (Moscow) to the Foreign Office[1]

Tel. No. 1551 *Immediate Confidential*   MOSCOW, 23 August 1961
                                                                    D. 6.43 p.m.
                                                                    R. 7.25 p.m.

Repeated for information Priority to Washington, Paris, Bonn, UKDEL NATO and Berlin.

Berlin.
Following is unofficial translation of Soviet Note delivered today at 14.20 hours GMT. The United States and French Embassies have received similar notes.
Begins:
The Ministry of Foreign Affairs of the U.S.S.R. present their compliments to the British Embassy and, on instructions from the Soviet Government, state the following.

2. The Soviet Government have more than once drawn the attention of the British Government to the unlawful and inadmissible interference by the FRG into the affairs of West Berlin. It is generally known that West Berlin does not constitute a part of the FRG and that the competence of the latter's authorities cannot extend to it. This is admitted by the Governments of the Western Powers.

3. Nevertheless, the British Government has not taken due steps to avert the provocative activity of certain circles of the FRG in West Berlin. With the connivance of the occupying organs of the three Powers in West Berlin this activity not only has not stopped, but of late, especially in connexion with the proposal for an urgent peaceful settlement with Germany and the solution on this basis of the question of West Berlin, has abruptly intensified. This activity is attaining such proportions as to create a danger of violation of peace and tranquillity in this area.

4. In West Berlin for a long period Bonn's Minister for so called all-German questions, Lemmer, has been operating. He has set up his residence there, in which provocations of various kinds are being prepared and from which the direction of subversive work against the DDR and other Socialist countries is being exercised. Revanchistes, extremists, subverters, spies and saboteurs of all kinds are being sent from the FRG to West Berlin. In order to send them there the Western Powers are using the

---

[1] DBPO Ser. 3 Vol. 6 No. 325; CG 1381/12.

air corridors as well. Thus the United States, Britain and France are patently abusing their position in West Berlin, profiting from the absence of control on the air communications. As a result there has been gross violation of the agreement reached in 1945 under which, as is well known, air corridors were assigned to the three Western Powers, temporarily, for the supplying of the needs of their military garrisons, not for the subversive and revanchist aims of West German militarism and not for the conducting of those subversive actions which are being demonstratively carried out before the eyes of the whole world, including the Germans themselves, by West German figures who have recently been turning up almost daily in West Berlin. By the air corridors to West Berlin, official representatives of the Government and Bundestag of the FRG are also arriving who set off directly from the airport on demonstrative tours of 'inspection' round the city and make provocative hostile statements against the DDR and the Soviet Union. Last week alone the Chairman of the Bundestag of the FRG, Gerstenmaiern, the Chairman of the CDU/CSU Party in the Bundestag, Krone, the Chairman of the SDP, Ollenhauer, the Chairman of the FDP, Mende, and others, assembled there. Their arrival was accompanied by the organization of rallies and demonstrations at which calls for aggression against peace-loving neighbouring States and for reprisals against the democratic forces of West Berlin were openly proclaimed.

5. The intensified intrigues of the ruling circles of the FRG in West Berlin are testimony of their strivings intentionally to render the situation in this area more acute so as to evoke complications and conflicts and to attempt to bring the Western Powers into collision with the Soviet Union to the advantage of the West German militarists and revanchistes. All this is taking place before the eyes and with the benevolent support of the Occupation Authorities of the three Powers in West Berlin who, it would seem, ought to have taken into account the dangerous consequences of the above-mentioned provocative activity of those circles of the FRG who have founded their policy on ideas of revanche.

6. In continuing to connive at the interference of the authorities of the FRG into the affairs of West Berlin and at the utilization of the territory of the city for acts of international provocation, the Government of Great Britain bears full responsibility for the possible consequences.

7. The Government of the USSR insists that the Government of Great Britain, which is exercising at the present time occupation functions in West Berlin, should forthwith take steps to terminate the unlawful and provocative activities of the FRG in this city.

39

Telegram from Maj-Gen Sir R. Delacombe (BMG Berlin) to the Foreign Office[1]

Tel. No. 320 *Immediate Confidential*   BERLIN, 23 August 1961
                                                                            D: 8.45 p.m.
                                                                            R: 8.58 p.m.

Addressed to Bonn No. 211, repeated for information Immediate to Foreign Office, Washington, HQ BAOR, and Priority to UKDEL NATO.

My telegram No. 207: Berlin.

The Commandants and their staffs met this morning to discuss the new situation created by the latest East German restrictions on movement within Berlin. They agreed as a first step on the terms of a Press release, the text of which is contained in my telegram No. 208.

2. It was agreed that there could be no question of complying with the East German instructions to remain a hundred metres from the sector border. The Commandants, therefore, agreed that Allied troops should show the flag immediately within the hundred metre belt, though it is not intended at present that Allied forces should be positioned there permanently. Accordingly, a company of British troops, supported by armoured personnel carriers, were despatched this morning to the hundred metre belt between the British and Soviet sectors, and the Allies have taken similar action.

3. Brandt then joined the meeting. He was shown the text of the Press statement, and expressed the Senate's gratitude for the Allied intention to display a military presence within the hundred metres belt. He pointed out that observation of the East German order would require the evacuation of many houses at present occupied by West Berliners that happened to lie within a hundred metres of the sector border.

4. Brandt then asked that the Commandants should authorise the following actions which the Senate considered desirable:

(*a*) authority should be given to the West Berlin Police to shut the offices, in West Berlin when installed, issuing permits for East Berlin (paragraph 1 of my telegram No. 207). The Senate was of the opinion that it was necessary to close these offices even though it would interfere with the few possibilities remaining for West Berliners to go to East Berlin;

---

[1] DBPO Ser. 3 Vol. 6 No. 326; CG 10113/74.

(*b*) the Senate wished to obtain authority from the Allies to establish control points at the sector crossing points and to turn back undesirable East Germans. He seemed to have in mind SED party functionaries, government officials etc. As to a possible control on non-Germans entering West Berlin, Brandt indicated that he preferred that a measure of this sort should be executed by the Allies;

(*c*) the DDR had now closed four SPD offices in East Berlin. Brandt said that his party would this afternoon probably decide to dissolve SPD branches in East Berlin. He asked that in these circumstances the Allies should examine whether some action against the SED in West Berlin, (permitted under terms of a 1946 BK/O) should now be taken. In this connexion, he admitted that there was little sign of SED activity in West Berlin and thought that they had gone underground.

5. Brandt added that on the instruction of the Federal Government Leopold, of the Trustee Office for Interzonal Trade, was this morning calling on Behrendt to inform him that the latest actions of the DDR could hardly fail to have an effect on last December's agreement.

6. See my immediately following telegram.

Telegram from Sir H. Caccia (Washington) to the Foreign Office[1]

Tel. No. 2063 *Immediate Secret*   WASHINGTON, 25 August 1961
                                                         D. 7.55 p.m.
                                                         R. 8.20 p.m.

Repeated for information to Moscow, Bonn, Paris, UKDEL NATO and Berlin.

My telegrams Nos. 2043 and 2044: Berlin Air Access.

The French draft having arrived was remitted, together with the draft in my telegram No. 2044, to a quadripartite group. The resulting draft, which was accepted this morning by the Ambassadorial Group, is in my immediately following telegram. We were able to work in the substance of most of paragraphs 2 and 3 of your telegram No. 5809.

2. It was agreed that the co-ordination of any minor amendments which Governments might wish to suggest should be done tripartitely in Moscow. The three Ambassadors should be authorized to deliver identical Notes as soon as possible, preferably tomorrow, Saturday, morning. The texts would be released to the press in capitals eight hours later, e.g. if delivered at 10 a.m. Moscow time, they would be released at 10 a.m. Washington time.

3. It was also agreed that our three representatives at NATO should forthwith circulate the text to their colleagues.

---

[1] DBPO Ser. 3 Vol. 6 No. 329; CG 1381/13.

Telegram from Sir H. Caccia (Washington) to the Foreign Office[1]

Tel. No. 2064 *Immediate Secret*   WASHINGTON, 25 August 1961
                                                                        D. 8.49 p.m.
                                                                        R. 10.47 p.m.

Repeated for information to Moscow, UKDEL NATO, Bonn, Berlin and Paris.

My immediately preceding telegram.

The following is English text:

[Standard opening paragraph with reference to the Soviet Government's Note of August 23].

The Government of the Soviet Union objects in its Note to the use by the Western Allies of their air corridors to Berlin. Her Majesty's Government must protest strongly against the suggestion that the purposes for which the Western Allies use the air corridors are within the competence of the Soviet Union. These corridors were established in 1945 by decision of the Four Power Allied Control Council as the manner in which the unrestricted right of air access to Berlin would be exercised by the Western Powers. There has never been any limitation whatsoever placed upon their use by the aircraft of the Western Powers. Her Majesty's Government will hold the Government of the Soviet Union responsible for any interference with the safety of these aircraft in the corridors.

The Government of the USSR in its Note accuses the Western Powers of violating the Four-Power Agreements of 1945. In particular, it reproaches them for 'their tolerance with respect to the interference of the authorities of the Federal Republic of Germany in the affairs of West Berlin and in regard to the use of the territory of that city for international provocations . . .' and insists 'that the Government of Great Britain, which at present exercises occupation functions in West Berlin, take immediate action to stop the illegal and provocative activities of the Federal Republic of Germany in that city.'

This demand is at the very least surprising. Indeed, since the night of August 12 to 13 the authorities of East Germany, with the concurrence of the Soviet Union, as the Note of the Soviet Government dated August 18 attests, have not ceased taking unilateral measures which do precisely violate the Four-Power Agreements and the freedom of movement within

---

[1] DBPO Ser. 3 Vol. 6 No. 330; CG 1381/13.

the city of Berlin. First they erected barricades, strengthened from day to day, to stop the traffic from East to West, in order, in fact, to put an end to the increasing exodus of refugees. For some days the same authorities have been attempting to establish unilateral and arbitrary control over access to East Berlin by the inhabitants of West Berlin and the Federal Republic of Germany. And they have just limited to a single point the possibilities of movement of the allies from West to East. Moreover, the inhabitants of East Berlin who worked in West Berlin have been denied the pursuit of their occupations. If there are 'illegal and provocative activities', they are certainly those of the authorities of East Germany in taking such measures and, as the British Note delivered to the Soviet Government on July 17 stated, if there is a crisis in Berlin, it is certainly the doing of the Soviet Union. Did not the number of refugees increase considerably from the day on which the Soviet Government made apparent the imminence of the implementation of its plan for a separate 'Peace' Treaty and a 'Free City'?

The Soviet Government protests against the presence in West Berlin of personalities from the Federal Republic, such as, for example; 'Mr Gerstenmeier, the President of the Bundestag of the Federal Republic of Germany; Mr Krone, the Chairman of the Fraction of the Christian Democratic Party; Mr Ollenhauer, the President of the Socialist Party, etc. . . .' Her Majesty's Government does not understand the position of the Soviet Government. West Berlin has a wide variety of ties with the Federal Republic that are in no way incompatible with the Four-Power status of Berlin. These accusations are all the more inadmissible since, for a long time and even quite recently, the Soviet Union as well as the East German authorities have been trying to integrate East Berlin completely into East Germany by isolating it from the outside and attempting to make it the capital of East Germany.

The fundamental fact is that the whole of Berlin has a quadripartite status. Her Majesty's Government note that the Soviet Government explicitly recognizes the rights and responsibilities of the Western Powers in Berlin. Unlike the Soviet Government, the Western Powers have always taken great care to see that the special status of the city as a whole is protected and preserved in accordance with Four Power Agreements. The Western Powers have established thorough procedures and safeguards for this purpose and the Soviet Government is well aware of this. Her Majesty's Government are willing as always to consider any legitimate complaints which the Soviet Union may put forward, but the allegations in the Soviet Note are pure fantasy.

Accordingly, it is up to the Soviet Union and not Her Majesty's Government to take measures to allay the state of tension and unrest which has developed in Berlin. The whole world will be concerned at the scarcely veiled threat of aggression against the allied air routes to and from West Berlin. Her Majesty's Government must serve a solemn warning to the Soviet Union that interference by the Soviet Government or its East German regime with free access to Berlin would have the most serious consequences for which it would bear full responsibility.

Telegram from Sir C. Steel (Bonn) to the Foreign Office[1]

Tel. No. 846 *Immediate Secret*   BONN, 26 August 1961
D: 12.25 p.m.
R: 12.36 p.m.

Following personal for Shuckburgh.

You asked me yesterday if I thought that the Soviet Note about the air corridors had produced a new situation. I said I thought not. My reasons are as follows.

I am convinced that the sealing of the Soviet sector of Berlin was not an original part of Khrushchev's programme. It has, however, been fitted into the pattern and has probably had a more encouraging impact from his point of view than he expected. The West Berliners and West Germans, instead of hailing the DDR action as a confession of defeat for Communism, stupidly bemoaned it as a Western defeat and blamed everything on their allies. But this whole incident should not obscure the fact that Khrushchev has for months been trying to frighten and confuse us all by a steady stream of Notes, speeches and interviews which seem to me all designed to have us properly dithering as the deadline of the Communist Party Congress approaches. He no doubt hopes to get us into negotiations when we are thoroughly confused and at odds with each other, but if we assume, as we always have, and I think must, that he does not want a war I would not expect his bluster to extend to any incident liable to produce a real spark (compare the great care taken over Western interests on August 13). I would estimate that any physical action in the air corridor would appear to him as being about the most dangerous that he could take since it would be almost bound to result in loss of life and lead to rapid escalation. In brief, I feel convinced that the Note about the corridors is

(*a*) part of the general propaganda build-up, and

(*b*) designed to create a new factitious grievance with an eye to coming negotiations.

3.[sic] As I have said above, all this is predicated on the theory that Khrushchev does not want war. If we are going to question this we ought radically to re-think our whole policy.

---

[1] DBPO Ser. 3 Vol. 6 No. 331; CG 1381/52.

43

Memorandum by the Earl of Home for the Cabinet[1]

C(61)132 *Secret*   FOREIGN OFFICE, 1 September 1961

Berlin

My colleagues will wish to have an account of the present situation regarding Berlin.

The Situation

2. On 12th August the sector border between East and West Berlin was closed by the East German authorities in order to stop the westward flow of refugees which had begun to run at the rate of about a thousand a day. Ten days later, on 22nd August, severe restrictions were placed on the movement of West Germans and West Berliners in both directions across the sector border. Allied personnel and foreigners were also affected to some extent. Throughout these actions the East Germans took care to avoid interference with communications between West Berlin and West Germany and there seemed to be a careful policy of not attacking Allied rights as such. However, on 23rd August the Soviet Government addressed a Note to the Three Powers protesting against Allied 'misuse' of the air corridors, thus giving grounds for the fear that they intended to begin to interfere with this traffic.

3. These moves led to a sharp rise in international tension and it was legitimate to speculate whether Mr Khrushchev might have decided to advance the programme which he had hitherto set, which was to 'settle' the Berlin problem before the end of the year by concluding a separate peace treaty with East Germany. General de Gaulle took the view that the Note on abuse of the air corridors was so sinister that he wanted to issue a ringing challenge to Mr Khrushchev then and there calling upon him to choose between peace and war. We (and I think all the other Allies) took a different view, which seems so far to have been justified by the event. We thought it more probable that the measures taken by the East German authorities had been in the first instance forced on them by the increase in the flow of refugees and the deteriorating situation in East Germany; and that after the initial step the Soviets, finding that the Western reaction was not too drastic, had decided to allow further minor acts of restriction and to make further threats, primarily as a means of strengthening their position for an eventual negotiation. Other moves of a similar character may well follow in the weeks to come, in order to increase the pressures

---

[1] DBPO Ser. 3, Vol. 6, No. 332; C(61)132; CAB 129/102.

on the West and to give the Soviet negotiators points which they can later 'concede'. It is possible, for example, that the inter-zonal trade agreement may break down and that there may be interference with West Berlin's trade and harassment of its communications with the West.

4. The people of East Germany are now effectively caged in and despite reports of widespread discontent there is no sign of any effective movement of resistance. We have of course been extremely careful not to encourage any such movement as it would certainly be ruthlessly suppressed, a process which would cause the gravest situation on the borders of East and West Germany. The Federal Government, too, have been very cautious over this. West Berlin is now almost wholly isolated from East Berlin and from the surrounding *Deutsche Demokratische Republik* (DDR). The 'shop window' has its blinds down and the escape route or safety valve from East Germany is closed. To this extent therefore West Berlin is less dangerous to East Germany than it was and at least one of the main Soviet complaints about the existence of free communications between West Berlin and the Federal Republic (namely, that it was used to carry refugees) has been removed. This could make the negotiation of a settlement easier. Against this, however, the local situation in Berlin itself is certainly fraught with danger and the Russians may at any time renew their protests that our aircraft carry 'revanchist' West Germans and demand that the practice be stopped under the threat of closure.

Western Policy
(*a*) *Move Towards Negotiation*

5. Throughout these events and since the Paris meeting of Western Foreign Ministers in July, we have been trying to obtain Four-Power agreement on a move towards negotiation with the Soviet Union. This was one part of the two-barrelled policy outlined by the United States Secretary of State, Mr Rusk, on behalf of the President at Paris—namely a policy of building up military strength on the one hand and being ready to negotiate on the other. My colleagues should understand the significance of the adoption of this policy by President Kennedy. Hitherto the idea of 'negotiating' over Berlin had been considered as almost equivalent to treason and much obloquy had been cast on Her Majesty's Government by American and other commentators for our alleged inclination towards it. At Paris not only did Mr Rusk say that President Kennedy was determined to negotiate, but he insisted that a public move to this end must be made before the end of August. Furthermore the American Delegation stated in terms that, although they considered the freedom of West Berlin and the maintenance of the Allied position there to be vital American interests, they were not prepared to go to war for the reunification of

Germany or over theoretical issues relating to the recognition of the DDR (e.g., who stamps the documents, & c.). At the same time Mr Rusk made it clear that the President did not support plans (which had been giving us so much concern over the previous year) for large-scale operations up the autobahn in the event of interference with Allied access.

6. We naturally welcomed wholeheartedly this evolution of American thinking on the Berlin problem and tried to give our full support to both barrels of their policy. On the negotiation side we have consistently supported the President's desire for a public move in this direction to be made before 1st September. There has been dogged opposition from General de Gaulle. By the time my colleagues read this paper some public statement will, I trust, have been made by the United States Government and we shall have supported it; but I cannot yet tell whether the French will consent to be associated with it.

(*b*) *The Build-up of Strength*

7. The build-up of strength has been more difficult for us. I do not think that we can contest the reasoning behind American policy. Mr Khrushchev is in an arrogant bullying mood and if he thought he could get away with no opposition he would end the life of West Berlin now. The Americans have therefore advocated a substantial increase in the conventional power of the North Atlantic Alliance, for two purposes, namely (*a*) as a means of pressure on Mr Khrushchev pending negotiations, and (*b*) in order to give the Alliance a wide range of military counter-action for use as a last resort (and after trying an airlift and non-military counter-measures) if all kinds of negotiations, including the United Nations, fail. We accepted this and I told my colleagues in Paris that Her Majesty's Government were willing to send certain units (including a Surface-to-Air Guided Weapons regiment) to Germany; to retain existing fighter squadrons in Germany and send additional fighter aircraft; to earmark a squadron of Canberra aircraft with nuclear capacity; and to organise forces in the United Kingdom into a division including armour which would be held available for reinforcement in Europe. Under arrangements made by the Minister of Defence, these steps have since been announced by stages and are being put into effect. A small number of additional armoured vehicles has also been sent to Berlin.

8. These measures have been just enough to prevent our being criticised by our Allies up to the present. They do not, however, represent a significant increase in the effective strength of the British Army of the Rhine (BAOR) and they do not suffice to meet requests which are now being addressed to us (and to the other members of the Alliance) by the Supreme Allied Commander, Europe, for additional military effort. On the other hand, I understand that there is very little more we can do without

calling up reserves and introducing some form of compulsory military service. This is one of the main problems confronting us at present.

(*c*) *Economic Counter-Measures*

9. The American Memorandum of 21st July (C. (61) 117) proposed that the Alliance should make a number of advance preparations in all fields, so as to be able to meet any eventuality with a choice of a wide range of options, and with military action as a last resort. It argued that in the event of blockage of our access to Berlin we should be prepared to take severe economic counter-measures against the Soviet bloc in support of an air-lift and political and diplomatic activity. The idea was that we might persuade the Russians to desist from their action by means short of military action leading ultimately to all-out war. This was very close to the policy already approved by the Defence Committee in June.

10. These proposals were discussed in Paris. The result was agreement that in the event of complete blockage of military and civilian access, by air or ground, significant economic counter-measures amounting to a total economic embargo would have to be applied. It was also agreed that appropriate measures to meet situations short of a complete blockage should be studied in Washington; and that the four Governments would immediately undertake the necessary legislative and administrative dispositions required to enable them to act promptly on all these measures if and when it was agreed to put them into effect. Finally, it was agreed that these proposals should be put to the North Atlantic Alliance, so that other members of the Alliance could make similar plans, since few of the measures in question would be of any value unless applied by the Alliance as a whole.

11. Work is going ahead very fast in Washington, and will soon begin to develop rapidly in the Alliance. Unless we can clear our own minds without delay we shall not be in a position to influence this. We have made it clear, both in Washington and in the Alliance, that economic counter-measures, and especially those which may have an effect on sterling, present special difficulties for us. We cannot afford to seem to our Allies reluctant to play our full part in this field. The Americans see economic counter-measures as an essential element in avoiding all-out war if a crisis becomes serious, and we have accepted this. If we (and other members of the Alliance) show unwillingness to take these measures, the Americans may well return to theories of military measures at an earlier stage, acting alone if necessary. This would be infinitely more disastrous to us than the imposition of economic measures. The Annex to this paper contains a summary of the more important measures now being discussed in Washington and gives a commentary on them.

The Future

12. It is quite clear that we are going to have negotiation of some sort with the Soviet Union before the end of the year. It will be very tough and difficult. Mr Khrushchev is in a thoroughly overweaning and dangerous frame of mind and believes that he has, in Berlin, an issue over which all the local factors are favourable to him. The question is whether he can be persuaded, by the resolute conduct, the unity and growing strength of the Alliance, that he cannot obtain the whole of his demands but must be content with a settlement which does not humiliate the West. The military build-up has one obvious danger. It creates a crisis atmosphere which in itself makes negotiation more difficult and concessions in negotiation more of a defeat. But in my view, the measures taken by President Kennedy to increase American preparedness are right and necessary as part of his preparations for a negotiation and the Allies ought to do whatever they can to match this and to show their support of the North Atlantic Alliance. Her Majesty's Government have an important role of leadership in this. We are very close to the Americans on the whole problem and even the Federal German Chancellor, Dr Adenauer, whose attitude, despite coming elections, has been rational and cautious. Our contribution so far has been very modest. The Minister of Defence will be able to advise what if any more can be done.

Basis for Negotiation

13. On what basis shall we negotiate? This is now the central problem which we must face in the coming weeks and which I shall be discussing with my three colleagues at the meeting for Western Foreign Ministers which has now been called for 14th September in Washington. It has hitherto been assumed that the opening position which the West would have to adopt in any negotiation would be based on the Western Peace Plan of 1959 suitably brought up to date. I am not at all sure that this is now the right tactic. There is something to be said for avoiding the inevitable recriminations of a debate about self-determination and reunification and concentrating negotiation on the narrowest front, namely that of Allied presence and uninterrupted access. I tried to avoid discussing the substance of the Berlin problem before the German elections because I believe that after they are safely elected a German Government will be less rigid in their approach to a settlement. But under strong pressure from the Americans I have agreed to a meeting on 14th September.

14. My colleagues will recall an earlier paper (C. (61) 116) in which I set down some of the ingredients which would have to go into a package settlement. The solution which will emerge must lie somewhere between a 'free city of West Berlin' on the lines advocated by Mr Khrushchev (a

solution which I fear would merely lead to the early absorption of the city by the Communist bloc) and a Western-controlled West Berlin in which we retain our troops and our rights of access and are able effectively to protect the freedom of the West Berliners.

15. I will, of course, report to the Cabinet after the Washington meeting, the intention of this paper being to bring the events of the last few weeks together for the convenience of my colleagues.

H[OME]

Annex

Economic Countermeasures

It was agreed in Paris that in the event of a complete blockage of military and civilian access, by air or ground, significant economic countermeasures amounting to a total economic embargo would have to be employed against the Soviet bloc (China is not included). This is understood to mean that in the contingency envisaged countries in the North Atlantic Alliance would all begin to mount significant economic countermeasures along with an airlift, diplomatic activity and the mobilisation of conventional forces. By the time a decision was taken to use these forces a wide range of countermeasures would progressively have been employed and when that decision was taken all countries would fill the remaining gaps to make up a total embargo.

2. The following are the more important countermeasures suggested in the contingency of a complete blockage:

(*a*) extend export control measures against Soviet bloc countries, including a selective embargo leading up to (*e*) below;

(*b*) suspend existing contracts to charter shipping to Soviet bloc countries;

(*c*) close allied ports and airports to Soviet bloc shipping and civil aircraft;

(*d*) terminate trade agreement involving Soviet bloc members;

(*e*) institute total trade embargo, i.e., complete denial by members of the Alliance of all their exports to and imports from Soviet bloc countries;

(*f*) cut off all financial facilities from members of the Alliance to the Soviet Union and other Soviet bloc members;

(*g*) freeze all Soviet bloc financial assets under the jurisdiction of the Alliance Powers.

It was also agreed that appropriate economic measures to meet situations short of a complete blockage should be studied.

3. A complete economic embargo against the Soviet bloc would cause much greater damage to the West than to the East. The Soviet Union itself

would be affected only to the extent that the rate of its future development would be reduced, and that not for some two or three years. Its current standard of living would not be affected. The only Soviet bloc countries to feel the pinch would be East Germany and Poland.

4. The West, on the other hand, would be vulnerable to the effect of its own measures and to any retaliatory economic measures which Soviet bloc Governments might impose. For most of the countries of the West these boomerang effects might not be serious but the effects on the interests of some of them, including the United Kingdom, could be grave and relatively quick. For example, the loss of our imports of Soviet soft wood and manganese would compel us to turn to other expensive markets. Our export trade with the Soviet bloc is of the order of £100 millions a year (direct exports) and £35 millions a year (re-exports). As far as shipping is concerned, it is clear that countries in the Alliance with much more shipping at stake are likely to suffer very much greater harm than the Soviet bloc once each side starts to interfere with the other's shipping. The long-term effects on the United Kingdom shipping interests would be particularly serious.

5. Moreover, in the view of the Treasury the freezing of Soviet bloc assets would involve grave consequences for sterling, even apart from the adverse effects of the Berlin situation generally. The damage would be particularly serious superimposed on our present economic difficulties. If the embargo were not in the event followed by war we should emerge with our financial and economic strength greatly weakened. The Bank of England wish to record that they are completely and utterly opposed to the freezing of sterling balances. If this was coincident with the outbreak of war it could be accepted, but any suggestion that assets should be frozen during a period of negotiations perhaps prior to war is regarded by the Bank of England as doing the greatest disservice to sterling at a time when it is perhaps on the point of recovery from a severe setback.

6. The situation envisaged in Paris was that access to Berlin, both civilian and military, would be completely blocked; in such circumstances, allied forces would be locked up in Berlin and it would be apparent that the Soviet Union, despite all our efforts, was determined to squeeze Berlin out altogether. War would therefore be imminent. In this very grave contingency, the dangers to sterling and to our trade which would follow from the more severe of the countermeasures contemplated would have to be accepted. If war did not ensue, the grave consequences described in the preceding paragraph would have to be set against the advantages of having avoided armed conflict.

7. We should obtain little relief by attempting to apply the embargo to selected items only. The Soviet bloc might retaliate by stopping its

purchases of other items from us or its own exports of the items which we can least afford to lose. Moreover, we could not in any case afford to make purchases from the Soviet bloc if we had substantially reduced our exports, since this would involve us directly or indirectly in net gold payments.

8. It has been suggested that the most effective means of leading up to a total embargo, with the maximum of adverse effects on the Soviet bloc as compared with the West and the United Kingdom in particular, would be to begin by imposing restrictions on trade with East Germany only. On balance such a measure would hurt East Germany much more than it hurt countries in the Alliance. Our representatives in Washington have therefore been instructed to suggest such a course as a countermeasure to be applied if necessary at a relatively early stage, the application of the more severe measures against the Soviet bloc as a whole being withheld to the very last stage. The initial reaction of the Americans is unfavourable, but an opportunity will shortly occur to put our suggestions at a higher level, if this seems desirable.

44

Mr McDermott (BMG Berlin) to Sir C. Steel (Bonn)[1]

No. 1 *Confidential*   BERLIN, 3 January 1962
                                                        R. 10 January 1962

Sir,

I have the honour to submit my report on West Berlin for the period from the 1st of June to the 1st of December, 1961, together with a calendar of the main events. The period of review is dominated by the measures taken by the East German authorities on August 13 and afterwards to seal off West Berlin from the DDR. In General Delacombe's despatch No. E(S)15 of the 27th November he reviewed the main events leading up to August 13 and described the East German measures in detail. I therefore do not propose to go over the same ground again in this despatch although some degree of repetition is inescapable.

2. The East German measures taken in August deprived West Berlin of its triple role as escape hatch for refugees from the DDR, show window of Western democracy and meeting place for both East and West Germans. They also threw into sharp relief the facts that West Berlin was an island fortress with tenuous lifelines to the West; and that in the last resort its protectors were bound to think more of maintaining their position than restoring the quadripartite status in East Berlin. One of the consequences of these events was a drop in the morale of the population of West Berlin and a decline in their confidence in Allied firmness and determination to resist the Communist advance, though there was some recovery in both respects towards the end of the period.

3. As General Delacombe wrote in his despatch No. 10 of the 27th of June 1961, the announcement that President Kennedy and Mr Khrushchev would meet in Vienna at the beginning of June produced a detectable upsurge of apprehension among the West Berliners, who entered June wary of what the rest of the year might hold for them. In the event, the reaction in West Berlin to the course of the meeting in Vienna was a mixture of relief that the President had not given anything away and foreboding that, by handing his memorandum to President Kennedy on June 4, Mr Khrushchev had put the West on notice that the Soviet Union would resume its pressure for a West Berlin solution that would turn it into a 'free city' in the Communist sense of the term. When a period of relative quiet followed some West Berliners no doubt hoped that the thunder-cloud on the horizon would dissolve before assuming the proportions of a direct

---

[1] CG 1017/8.

menace, as it had so often done since November 1958. This perhaps might have been the case had not events in East Germany precipitated matters more quickly than even the pessimists had predicted. To the implied threats in Mr Khrushchev's Vienna memorandum the East German authorities added their own. They elaborated on the Soviet demand for the establishment of a 'free city' in West Berlin. They also stepped up the immediate pressure on the population of the DDR, and introduced campaigns against refugees and against the so-called *Grenzgaenger* (East Germans and East Berliners working in West Berlin). The result was a spectacular rise in the number of refugees. In order to control a situation which was in danger of getting completely out of hand the authorities in the DDR took the momentous steps on August 13 and afterwards which resulted in the sealing off of West Berlin from East Berlin and the rest of the Soviet Zone by the erection of a wall and barbed wire barricades around the Western sectors and the establishment of a virtual prohibition on movement between West Berlin and the surrounding territory. The fact that West Germans and foreigners, including members of the Allied forces in West Berlin, were still permitted to move between East and West Berlin merely underlined the extent to which these measures completed the division of Berlin into two separate cities.

4. The reaction in West Berlin to the East German measures was a complex one, the aftereffects of which are still to be observed. To begin with, there was a combination of spontaneous anger and resentment that made itself felt in spirited but ineffective demonstrations on the border between West and East Berlin. These led to minor clashes with the East German *Volkspolizei* and, on a different level, with West Berlin policemen trying to maintain law and order and to prevent the demonstrators from becoming involved in serious incidents with the East German border personnel. It also led to the birth of a still widely held belief that the Allies had been at fault in not taking strong and positive action on and after August 13, such as knocking down the wall when it was being built. The protest against the measures of August 13 which the Western Commandants sent to the Soviet Commandant two days later provoked angry and frustrated comment in West Berlin and got perhaps the most critical reception of any Western action in Berlin for several years. The mood of the population was exemplified at a demonstration numbering several hundred thousand outside the Schoeneberg Rathaus on August 16 at which 'deeds not words' was the most prominent theme.

5. The crisis of confidence might have grown to serious proportions had not the Allies taken vigorous steps to prove their determination to stand firm in Berlin. On August 19 the Vice-President of the United States paid a flying visit to West Berlin, where he was greeted with a warmth and

enthusiasm that not even his oratory could dampen. He stayed to add his welcome to that given by the West Berliners to a US Army battle group that had been despatched from the Federal Republic to reinforce the garrison in West Berlin. A significant feature of Mr Johnson's visit was that he was accompanied by General Lucius D. Clay, at that time still a captain of industry. Since the days of the air lift General Clay has been to Berliners the personification of American determination and firmness, particularly where Berlin itself it concerned. It was widely noted that the greatest cheers during the Vice-President's visit were for General Clay. The arrival of reinforcements of armour for the British garrison also received a good reception in West Berlin. Then on August 23, in response to further East German decrees and in particular to an order warning people not to approach within 100 metres of the Sector border, the Western Commandants sent troops and armour right up to the border between West and East Berlin to establish an Allied military presence there.

6. These expressions of Western support were well timed and averted the immediate crisis of confidence. This was as well, for at about this time rumours and reports of impending Communist action against the air corridors gained currency. In the light of hindsight it is possible to say with some confidence that this was part of the now familiar Communist psychological warfare campaign against Berlin and did not presage real moves against the air corridors. Nevertheless, West Berliners were reminded once more of the uncomfortable fact that air access between Berlin and the Federal Republic was the only route over which the Communists had not as yet achieved a measure of direct control.

7. On September 19 General Clay arrived to take up his appointment as President Kennedy's personal representative, and highest ranking United States Government servant, in Berlin. The precise functions of the General have remained undefined. However, it is known that his responsibilities cover the field of the morale of the West Berliners; and General Clay appears by virtue of his personality and position to have enlarged this field to embrace the wide nexus of political and military matters which can to some extent or other be regarded as affecting West Berlin morale. Frankly, his activities have not always helped the functioning of the Allied Kommandatura, or indeed of the United States Commandant himself. There have also been occasions when the man whose presence in West Berlin was intended to stiffen the confidence of the population has functioned as an oversensitive instrument measuring real or imaginary changes in what the West Berliners think or expect of the Allies.

8. It is possible to trace General Clay's influence in the second major crisis in the period under review. This took place in the last week of

October at the Friedrichstrasse crossing point 'Checkpoint Charlie', in the American sector, which the DDR authorities had made the sole crossing point for non-Germans on August 23. There had already been sporadic attempts by the East German Volkspolizei to examine the identity documents of Allied Personnel crossing there. Such attempts had been resisted but, in accordance with their longstanding practice, British personnel in civilian dress were ready to show their identity documents to the Volkspolizei if necessary and had done so on a number of occasions. The Americans and the French on the other hand had equally venerable instructions that they were not to do so and had several times evaded the East German requirement only by having a Soviet officer summoned. Then in the evening of October 22 the American Deputy Commandant and Minister, Mr Lightner, tried to drive his own car into East Berlin to attend the opera. The Volkspolizei stopped him and asked to see his identity card which he refused to produce. The East Germans therefore refused to let him pass. The Soviets were called to the scene but declined to intervene as they had done in the past. The Americans then called up armed military police who escorted Mr Lightner through the Volkspolizei barriers for a brief trip in and out of East Berlin. On the following day the East Germans affirmed that they were entirely in the right in requiring persons in civilian clothes to establish their identity when entering East Berlin. That day and the following days the Americans mounted a series of probes into East Berlin. These began with an unsuccessful attempt by personnel in civilian clothes and in cars with official United States licence plates to enter East Berlin without having to identify themselves. They finished with the same personnel being escorted by armed United States military police through the East German checkpoint for a short sally into East Berlin, while American tanks deployed at the crossing point.

9. It was not to be expected that the Communists would endure this indefinitely. During the night of October 26 Soviet tanks and crews were sighted in the centre of East Berlin for the first time since June 1953. By the next evening, after another American probe, they were at Checkpoint Charlie and facing American tanks barely a hundred yards away. However, on the following morning first the Soviet and then the American tanks withdrew. Although both have remained within a few minutes' drive of Friedrichstrasse, they have not reappeared there since then.

10. It is generally recognised that one of the principal purposes of the America probes was to force a situation where the Soviets had no choice but to come into the open and thereby admit their responsibility for, and involvement in, events in the city and the hollowness of their statements about the sovereign independent powers of the DDR. This immediate aim was certainly attained when Soviet tanks appeared, and there is some

evidence that the Soviets were embarrassed at having to send their armour to the crossing point. Against this success must however be placed two less favourable results. In the first place, the logic of events compelled the Americans to continue to refuse to allow their personnel in civilian clothes to identify themselves to the Volkspolizei when entering East Berlin in vehicles. As the French have followed suit, it is only British civilian personnel who have driven into East Berlin since October. The disparity in Allied practice has been much criticised and much misunderstood; and it is not generally realised that the United States Deputy Commandant is firmly of the view—which he has expressed to me more than once—that the Americans would have done well to follow the sensible British practice long before questions of prestige made it impossible.

11. The second adverse consequence took some time to materialise. On November 19 the East Germans began to strengthen the wall of August 13 by the erection of a formidable anti-tank wall at the Brandenburg Gate, the Potsdamer Platz and selected vulnerable points along the central area of the border between East and West Berlin. By constructing these new anti-tank devices (which were extended in early December, outside the period covered by this despatch), the East Germans made it plain that as far as they were concerned the wall was there to stay. Furthermore they established themselves in a position where further American probes into East Berlin, perhaps to be carried out with tanks in an active and not merely support role, would be a major military operation in which it would be easy to portray the Americans as aggressors. The fact is, however, that from the military standpoint the border between East and West Berlin began to quieten down after American and Soviet tanks withdrew on October 27 and ceased for the time being to be an area of acute tension.

12. These events were not without their effect on West Berlin morale. It is my belief that the American action at Friedrichstrasse marked and perhaps assisted a change in the mood of the West Berliners. In August they had been highly critical of Allied inactivity. In September they had greeted the arrival of General Clay with an enthusiasm at least in part engendered by the belief that his presence would bring about a more forward policy. In October came the stimulation of the excitement at Friedrichstrasse, but at the same time the realization that, when all was said and done, not even the Americans were prepared to fight their way into East Berlin and that there were real dangers attendant on spectacular military demonstrations on the borders of West Berlin. By November there were signs that the verdict on the Allied action in August was undergoing some revision, though it was far from being reversed. It can be said that the traditional stability and good sense of the West Berliners, which was badly disturbed by the shock of August 13, has been to a large extent

restored, and with it an acute appreciation that in the last resort it is access to West Berlin from the Federal Republic, and not movement between East and West Berlin, on which the freedom and viability of the Western Sectors depend.

13. There are signs too that the lack of confidence in the future apparent since August is also diminishing. It is well known, if misleadingly reported, that after the 13th of August, the rate of emigration from West Berlin to the Federal Republic approximately trebled. The westward movement of persons and their goods was accompanied by some transfer of capital. The indications at the end of November suggest that these movements are levelling out. From the outset it was our view that these trends were but the natural symptoms of uncertainty and that they were of little absolute significance. What was important was to arrest the trend, and this could only be done by removing the underlying uncertainty about the future of the city. Provided this could be done before too long, the outward movement was unlikely to have much enduring importance either politically, economically or demographically. This remains our analysis. In the last resort the prosperity and future of Berlin depends from an economic as well as a political point of view, on security and confidence in the future. Only this climate can provide the right soil for effective external assistance, in particular financial and budgetary aid from the Federal Republic. The long-term conditions for achieving this fall outside the scope of this despatch, but in the short term it is probable that any prospect of reasonably successful international negotiations over Berlin will exert a beneficial influence on the morale and prosperity of the city. Conversely, any prolonged period of uncertainty and tension could inflict a grave set-back on the development of Berlin.

14. The coalition of the SPD and CDU in West Berlin reacted less to the Federal elections in the middle of September than to the pressure of events in Berlin itself. Although there was a good measure of pre-election acrimony, both elements in the Berlin coalition made common cause in attacking the Federal Government for its inactivity in respect of Berlin prior to September 17 and in lamenting the month of wrangling in Bonn following the elections that prevented the early formulation of the new Government's Berlin policy. The present position is that the coalition remains firmly established. There seems at present little likelihood that the Governing Mayor will forsake Berlin, and the real position of strength it gives him, for the quicksands of SPD politics in Bonn. He remains head and shoulders above his colleagues in the West Berlin Senate and has shown again that in a time of crisis he can be relied upon to counsel restraint and to perceive where West Berlin's vital interests lie.

I am sending copies of this despatch to Her Majesty's Representatives at Hamburg, Dusseldorf, Hannover, Frankfurt, Munich, Stuttgart and Bremen and to HQ BSSO, the C-in-C's Secretariat, HQ BAOR, the Joint Services Liaison Officer, Bonn and Research Department at the Foreign Office.

I have, etc.,
G.L. MCDERMOTT

45

Background brief by the Research Analysts[1]

FOREIGN AND COMMONWEALTH OFFICE, August 1986

Berlin—25 years of the Wall

On 13 August 1961 the East German authorities sealed off the Western sectors of Berlin from the Soviet sector with barricades. Residents of the Soviet sector and the German Democratic Republic (GDR), who were previously allowed freedom of movement between the Soviet and Western sectors, were forbidden to cross into West Berlin without a special permit. The barricades were subsequently replaced by the Berlin Wall; 25 years later Berlin remains a divided city.

Legal status of Berlin

At the end of the Second World War, Berlin was occupied jointly by the four wartime Allies—Britain, France, the United States and the Soviet Union. Agreement on the administration of the city and its division into sectors had earlier been reached in the European Advisory Commission (EAC), a body set up by the conference of British, American and Soviet Foreign Ministers held in Moscow in October 1943. France was invited to participate in this arrangement at the Yalta Conference of February 1945. Following the surrender of the German forces in May 1945, a joint declaration on the assumption by the Allies of supreme authority in Germany was signed in Berlin on 5 June 1945. Two accompanying statements were issued: that, among other things, 'the area of Greater Berlin will be occupied by the forces of each of the Four Powers'; and that the administration of the Greater Berlin area would be directed by an Allied Kommandatura (composed of the four military commandants). Berlin remains under Four-Power occupation. In accordance with Four-Power legislation, all German military activity in Berlin is forbidden.

Soviet intransigence and the Berlin blockade

One of the most important tasks of the Kommandatura, which assumed administration of the whole city in July 1945, was to arrange the election of a city council which in turn would draw up a Constitution. When elections for the Berlin City Assembly were held in October 1946, the Communist-dominated Socialist Unity Party polled only one-fifth of the

---

[1] The National Archives: FO 973/471.

votes. The Soviet authorities refused to cooperate with the other members of the Kommandatura and the Soviet commandant withdrew altogether on 1 July 1948. On 30 November 1948, the Soviet Union forcibly divided the municipal administration of Berlin by staging a raid by Communists on the Rathaus (town hall) situated in East Berlin. The elected majority of the city government was forced to withdraw to the US sector in the West, while the Soviet authorities set up a separate municipal administration in their sector (the East). This period was also marked by increasing Soviet interference with overland traffic to Berlin, culminating in the imposition by the Soviet authorities, in June 1948, of a total blockade of all surface access routes, intended to force the Western Allies to withdraw from the city.

The blockade was successfully countered by a massive airlift organised by the Western Allies. It was terminated by agreements of May and June 1949, and the Western Powers' right of access to the city was recognised by the USSR. The Soviet commandant in Berlin did not, however, return to the Kommandatura, which continues to operate on a Three-Power basis.

Second crisis and the Berlin Wall

On 5 May 1955 the Occupation regime was terminated in the Western zones of Germany (corresponding since 1949 to the Federal Republic of Germany, the FRG). This followed Soviet action on 27 March 1954 terminating the Occupation regime in the Soviet zone (corresponding since October 1949 to the German Democratic Republic, the GDR). The status of Berlin, however, remained unaffected by these changes.

In November 1958, the Soviet Government alleged that the Western Powers were using their position in West Berlin to pursue subversion against the Soviet Union and its allies, and that the basis of the agreements on Berlin had been destroyed. It proposed that West Berlin be made a 'demilitarised free city' and 'independent political unit within the structure of the State in whose territory it lies'. The Soviet Government specified a period of six months for negotiating the change in the position of Berlin; if this was not worked out it would transfer to the GDR the functions carried out by the Soviet authorities.

The ensuing crisis led to a Four-Power conference of Foreign Ministers in Geneva from May-August 1959. No agreement was reached because the Soviet delegation refused to give a clear acknowledgment of the Western Powers' existing rights and responsibilities with respect to Berlin. The crisis continued throughout 1959 and 1960, and in June 1961 Khrushchev gave President Kennedy an aide-memoire restating the Soviet position in even more uncompromising terms.

By August 1961 the tension arising from the Soviet demands was causing a marked increase in the number of refugees fleeing to West Berlin from the East. From September 1949, when the registration of refugees began, until the building of the wall on 13 August 1961, 2,691,270 refugees were registered. Many were skilled and qualified young people (3,400 doctors and over 17,000 engineers and technicians from 1954 onwards). Finally, the Berlin Wall was erected effectively ending freedom of movement between East and West Berlin and in flagrant violation of existing agreements on the quadripartite status of Berlin.

According to figures available up to 31 July 1986, there had, since the wall was built, been 74 confirmed cases of people killed trying to cross it to the West (57 having been shot); 115 had been wounded. There had been 4,909 escapes via the wall, including 554 members of the armed forces or police, and arrests at the wall numbered 3,141.

The Quadripartite Agreement

Following the improvement in East-West relations at the end of the 1960s, the Three Powers initiated talks with the Soviet Union. These began in March 1970 and resulted in the Quadripartite Agreement (QA) on Berlin, which was signed on 3 September 1971 and came into force in June 1972. The QA, and related arrangements negotiated by the FRG/West Berlin Senat and the GDR, sought an improvement in the political and practical problems arising from the situation in and around Berlin without affecting Berlin's legal status. In this, it has succeeded: it has made for faster and freer movement by road and rail between West Berlin and the FRG, eased restrictions on West Berliners visiting relatives in the GDR and East Berlin, and much reduced the Berlin problem as a source of tension the East-West relations.

Friction between the Western Powers and the Soviet Union arises from time to time over the exact interpretation of the QA. No accord, for example, could be reached on the territory actually covered by the agreement, which is described simply 'as the relevant area'. The Soviet Union asserts that the rights and responsibilities of the Four Powers regarding Berlin apply only in West Berlin, which it claims is a separate political entity. It says that its own sector is an integral part of the GDR, and its capital city; and that the boundary between the Eastern and Western sectors (the wall) is a State frontier between West Berlin and GDR. The Western Allies do not accept these Soviet assertions. Although the Western Allies have established their embassies to the GDR in East Berlin, and accepted that East Berlin is the GDR's 'seat of government', they have expressly stated that they have done so without prejudice to their legal position on Berlin.

The Western Allies make clear the continued existence of Four-Power rights throughout Berlin by sending daily army patrols (flag tours) around East Berlin. They still hold the USSR responsible for control in the Eastern sector and deal only with Soviet officials on matters concerning Berlin. This was demonstrated in May 1986, when the Western Allies protested to the Soviet Union over East German demands that diplomats accredited to the GDR should present their passports to East German guards and obtain GDR visas when crossing to West Berlin. The GDR withdrew the passport controls in June and instead issued new diplomatic identity cards.

FRG ties with Berlin

The Soviet Union has frequently disputed the provision in the QA covering ties between the Western sectors of Berlin and the FRG, which declares that such ties 'will be maintained and developed, taking into account that these sectors continue not to be a constituent part of the FRG and not to be governed by it'. The Soviet Union has consistently stressed that latter part of the formula, while playing down or ignoring the first half; it frequently protests about the inclusion of West Berliners in Federal German delegations at international conferences, about meetings of Federal bodies in or visits by Federal officials to the city, and about the extension to West Berlin by the FRG of treaties to which the FRG is a party. The Western Allies have pointed out that the activities complained of are permitted by the QA. During the Federal German Foreign Minister's visit to Moscow in July 1986, the Soviet Union concluded a bilateral agreement on scientific co-operation, which provides for participation by officials of Federal institutions in Berlin on a personal basis.

The Soviet Union has shown particular sensitivity over West Berlin's links with the European Community (EC), although the Treaty of Rome was extended to West Berlin with the approval of the three Western Powers in 1957. In doing so they entered a reservation of their rights and responsibilities, in accordance with standard procedure, ensuring that the city's legal status remains unaffected by developments in the EC. The Russians claim that, despite this reservation, the city's status is being undermined by its inclusion in the 'the process of Western integration'. They protested against the selection of three Members of Parliament from Berlin as part of the FRG quota in the European Parliament elections in June 1984. However, unlike MPs from East Berlin, who since 1981 have been directly elected to the GDR Volkskammer (People's Chamber), in blatant violation of Berlin's legal status, MPs from West Berlin in the Bundestag (Federal Parliament) are delegated by the Berlin House of Representatives and have limited voting rights.

Administration of West Berlin

West Berlin (population 1.85 million) is governed by an elected House of Representatives (currently 144 seats), with the executive power vested in the Senat, consisting of a Governing Mayor, a Deputy Mayor and a maximum of 16 Senators. Although the Western Allies have progressively devolved the business of running the city to the Senat, Berlin's legal status remains unaffected by these changes. The West Berlin authorities are required to consult the Allies, especially on matters of security and status, and in these fields in particular the Allies still exercise governmental powers. (For instance, when West Berlin decided to be linked to the Soviet natural gas pipeline from Siberia, the Allies insisted on the construction of an underground reservoir capable of storing a year's reserve supply.)

The process of devolution had begun in 1950, when a Constitution for Berlin, drafted by the elected city Council, was approved by the Kommandatura. The three Western commandants later issued a 'Declaration on Berlin', governing relations between the Allies and the local German authorities in Berlin, which came into force on 5 May 1955 and has remained unchanged.

Economic and social

Economic and social links between the FRG and West Berlin have ensured the city's development as an important industrial centre. The economy is dependent on, and integrated with, that of West Germany, to which it contributes 3.6 per cent of the Gross National Product (GNP). Eighty per cent of Berlin's exports go to the FRG, 18 per cent overseas and 2 per cent to the Eastern bloc (including the GDR). The electrical industry is the city's most important industrial sector, followed by mechanical engineering, chemicals, food and beverages, and tobacco. The city authorities have improved investment incentives and company tax is 22.5 per cent lower than in the FRG. The city has concentrated on attracting high technology, and over 300 high technology companies complement the 190 research institutes.

Terrorists and anarchist have attempted to use Berlin as a base, but their activities have been constrained—notwithstanding the bomb attack on a discotheque in April 1986, in which the Libyan People's Bureau was involved. A squatters' movement, exploited on occasion by militants to create violent confrontation with the police, persisted from 1980 until 1983. It was finally overcome by a strong and consistent line adopted by the Senat and the police. But the provision of adequate housing is a constant problem, exacerbated by the continuing influx into West Berlin of illegal immigrants from the Third World, seeking asylum. Just under 15,000 asylum-seekers registered in West Berlin between January and the end of June 1986. They arrive at Schönefeld airport, outside East Berlin, where the GDR authorities allow them to travel to the West without proper documentation.

750th anniversary

The 750th anniversary of the city of Berlin will be celebrated in 1987. The Queen will visit Berlin in May 1987 to mark the anniversary. The Western Allies are working closely with the Senat over arrangements for the celebrations. The GDR leadership says that it intends to underline the separate character of East and West Berlin, claiming that the 'progressive achievements and historic traditions are alive only in East Berlin'.

Despite the wall and the division of the city, however, Berlin survives as a symbol of Western freedoms. This it owes largely to the three Western Powers' joint commitment to uphold the city's legal status and to safeguard the rights of its people.

British Documents from the Archives

No. 1   Britain and the making of the Post-War World: The
         Potsdam Conference and beyond

No. 2   Preparing for Helsinki: The CSCE Multilateral
         Preparatory Talks

No. 3   Britain and the Berlin Crisis, 1961

Also available online: www.issuu.com/fcohistorians